CHARTBOOK
A Reference Grammar

UNDERSTANDING AND USING

English Grammar

FOURTH EDITION

PEARSON
Longman

Betty S. Azar
Stacy A. Hagen

Understanding and Using English Grammar, Fourth Edition Chartbook

Azar Associates: Shelley Hartle, Editor, and Sue Van Etten, Manager

Pearson Education, 10 Bank Street, White Plains, NY 10606

Staff credits: The people who made up the *Understanding and Using English Grammar, Fourth Edition, Chartbook* team, representing editorial, production, design, and manufacturing, are Dave Dickey, Christine Edmonds, Ann France, Amy McCormick, Robert Ruvo, and Ruth Voetmann.

Text composition: S4Carlisle Publishing Services
Text font: Helvetica
Illustrations: Don Martinetti—pages 1, 2 (top), 3, 9, 10, 12, 15, 18, 26, 30, 32, 34, 41, 49, 53, 64, 68, 76, 78, 96, 98, 110, 115; Chris Pavely—pages 2 (bottom), 16, 21, 24, 40, 44, 46, 50, 72, 74, 81, 99, 101, 105

ISBN 10: 0-13-205210-5
ISBN 13: 978-0-13-205210-8

Printed in the United States of America
7 8 9 10— V011 —15

Contents

Preface

Understanding and Using English Grammar Chartbook is a grammar reference for English language learners. It contains all the charts found in the student text *Understanding and Using English Grammar, fourth edition.* The information that English language learners want and need in order to communicate effectively is presented clearly, accurately, and concisely.

Intended as a reference tool for students and teachers alike, the *Chartbook* can be used alone or in conjunction with the *Workbook.* The practices in the *Workbook* are keyed to the charts in the *Chartbook.* Since the *Workbook* provides answers to all the practices, a *Chartbook* plus *Workbook* combination allows learners to study independently. More advanced students can work through much of the grammar on their own. They can investigate and correct their usage problems, expand their usage repertoire by doing self-study practices in the *Workbook,* and find answers to most of their grammar questions in the Chartbook.

Teachers and students may find the *Chartbook* plus *Workbook* combination especially useful in writing classes, in tutorials, or in rapid reviews in which grammar is not the main focus but needs attention.

Differences in structure and usage between American English and British English are noted throughout the text. The differences are few and relatively insignificant.

The *Teacher's Guide* contains background teaching notes for all the charts, as well as step-by-step instructions for in-class use. Included with the *Teacher's Guide* are ten beyond-the-book *PowerPoint* lessons, which highlight several key grammar structures.

Chapter 1
Overview of Verb Tenses

1-1 The Simple Tenses

This basic diagram will be used in all tense descriptions.

Tense	Examples	Meaning
Simple Present	(a) It *snows* in Alaska. (b) Tom *watches* TV every day.	In general, the simple present expresses events or situations that exist *always, usually, habitually;* they exist now, have existed in the past, and probably will exist in the future.
Simple Past	(c) It *snowed* yesterday. (d) Tom *watched* TV last night.	*At one particular time in the past,* this happened. It began and ended in the past.
Simple Future	(e) It *will snow* tomorrow. It *is going to snow* tomorrow. (f) Tom *will watch* TV tonight. Tom *is going to watch* TV tonight.	*At one particular time in the future,* this will happen.

1-2 The Progressive Tenses

Form: **be** + **-ing** (*present participle*)

Meaning: The progressive tenses* give the idea that an action is in progress during a particular time. The tenses say that an action *begins before, is in progress during, and continues after* another time or action.

Present Progressive	(a) Tom *is sleeping* right now.	It is now 11:00. Tom went to sleep at 10:00 tonight, and he is still asleep. His sleep began in the past, *is in progress at the present time,* and probably will continue.
Past Progressive	(b) Tom *was sleeping* when I arrived.	Tom went to sleep at 10:00 last night. I arrived at 11:00. He was still asleep. His sleep began before and *was in progress at a particular time in the past.* It continued after I arrived.
Future Progressive	(c) Tom *will be sleeping* when we arrive.	Tom will go to sleep at 10:00 tomorrow night. We will arrive at 11:00. The action of sleeping will begin before we arrive, and it *will be in progress at a particular time in the future.* Probably his sleep will continue.

*The progressive tenses are also called the "continuous" tenses: present continuous, past continuous, and future continuous.

They ***are waiting*** for the bus.
They ***were waiting*** for the bus five minutes ago.
They ***will be waiting*** for the bus for another ten minutes.

1-3 The Perfect Tenses

Form: **have** + *past participle*
Meaning: The perfect tenses all give the idea that one thing *happens before* another time or event.

Present Perfect	(a) Tom *has* already *eaten.*	Tom *finished* eating *sometime before now.* The exact time is not important.
Past Perfect	(b) Tom *had* already *eaten* when his friend arrived.	First Tom finished eating. Later his friend arrived. Tom's eating was completely *finished before another time in the past.*
Future Perfect	(c) Tom *will* already *have eaten* when his friend arrives.	First Tom will finish eating. Later his friend will arrive. Tom's eating will be completely *finished before another time in the future.*

1-4 The Perfect Progressive Tenses

Form: **have** + **been** + **-ing** (*present participle*)
Meaning: The perfect progressive tenses give the idea that one event is *in progress immediately before, up to, until another time or event.* The tenses are used to express the *duration* of the first event.

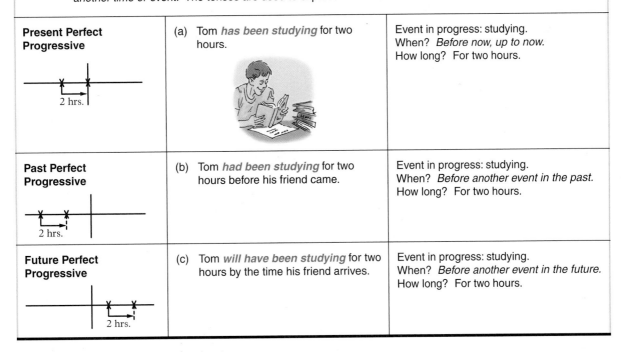

Present Perfect Progressive	(a) Tom *has been studying* for two hours.	Event in progress: studying. When? *Before now, up to now.* How long? For two hours.
Past Perfect Progressive	(b) Tom *had been studying* for two hours before his friend came.	Event in progress: studying. When? *Before another event in the past.* How long? For two hours.
Future Perfect Progressive	(c) Tom *will have been studying* for two hours by the time his friend arrives.	Event in progress: studying. When? *Before another event in the future.* How long? For two hours.

1-5 Summary Chart of Verb Tenses

Simple Present	Present Progressive
Tom *studies* every day.	Tom *is studying* right now.
Simple Past	**Past Progressive**
Tom *studied* last night.	Tom *was studying* when they came.
Simple Future	**Future Progressive**
Tom *will study* tomorrow. Tom *is going to study* tomorrow.	Tom *will be studying* when they come. Tom *is going to be studying* when they come.

Present Perfect	Present Perfect Progressive
Tom *has* already *studied* Chapter 1.	Tom *has been studying* for two hours.
Past Perfect	**Past Perfect Progressive**
Tom *had* already *studied* Chapter 1 before he began studying Chapter 2.	Tom *had been studying* for two hours before his friends came.
Future Perfect	**Future Perfect Progressive**
Tom *will* already *have studied* Chapter 4 before he studies Chapter 5.	Tom *will have been studying* for two hours by the time his roommate gets home.

1-6 Spelling of *-ing* and *-ed* Forms

(1) VERBS THAT END IN A CONSONANT AND *-e*	(a)	hope date injure	hoping dating injuring	hoped dated injured	*-ING* FORM: If the word ends in **-e**, drop the **-e** and add **-ing**.★ *-ED* FORM: If the word ends in a consonant and **-e**, just add **-d**.
(2) VERBS THAT END IN A VOWEL AND A CONSONANT	— ONE-SYLLABLE VERBS				

(1) VERBS THAT END IN A CONSONANT AND *-e*	(a) hope / hoping / hoped date / dating / dated injure / injuring / injured	*-ING* FORM: If the word ends in **-e**, drop the **-e** and add **-ing**.★ *-ED* FORM: If the word ends in a consonant and **-e**, just add **-d**.

(2) VERBS THAT END IN A VOWEL AND A CONSONANT	**ONE-SYLLABLE VERBS**
	(b) stop / stopping / stopped
	    rob / robbing / robbed
	(c) rain / raining / rained
	    fool / fooling / fooled
		(b) 1 vowel → 2 consonants★★
		
		(c) 2 vowels → 1 consonant

	TWO-SYLLABLE VERBS
	(d) listen / listening / listened
	    offer / offering / offered
	(e) begin / beginning / (began)
	    prefer / preferring / preferred
		(d) 1st syllable stressed → 1 consonant
		
		(e) 2nd syllable stressed → 2 consonants

(3) VERBS THAT END IN TWO CONSONANTS	(f) start / starting / started
	    fold / folding / folded
	    demand / demanding / demanded
		If the word ends in two consonants, just add the ending.

(4) VERBS THAT END IN *-y*	(g) enjoy / enjoying / enjoyed
	    pray / praying / prayed
	(h) study / studying / studied
	    try / trying / tried
	    reply / replying / replied
		If **-y** is preceded by a vowel, keep the **-y**.
		
		If **-y** is preceded by a consonant:
		-ING FORM: keep the **-y**; add **-ing**.
		-ED FORM: change **-y** to **-i**; add **-ed**.

(5) VERBS THAT END IN *-ie*	(i) die / dying / died lie / lying / lied	*-ING* FORM: Change **-ie** to **-y**; add **-ing**. *-ED* FORM: Add **-d**.

★Exception: If a verb ends in **-ee**, the final **-e** is not dropped: *seeing, agreeing, freeing.*

★★Exception: **-w** and **-x** are not doubled: *plow → plowed; fix → fixed.*

Chapter 2

Present and Past; Simple and Progressive

2-1 Simple Present

✗✗✗✗✗✗✗✗✗✗✗	(a) Water *consists* of hydrogen and oxygen. (b) The average person *breathes* 21,600 times a day. (c) The world *is* round.	The simple present says that something was true in the past, is true in the present, and will be true in the future. It expresses *general statements of fact and general truths.*
	(d) I *get* up at seven *every morning.* (e) I *always eat* a salad for lunch.	The simple present is used to express *habitual or everyday activities.*

2-2 Present Progressive

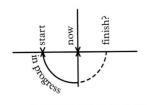	(f) The students *are sitting* at their desks right now. (g) I need an umbrella because it *is raining.* (h) I *am taking* five courses this semester.	The present progressive expresses an activity that is *in progress at the moment of speaking.* It is a temporary activity that began in the past, is continuing at present, and will probably end at some point in the future.

2-3 Non-Progressive Verbs

(a) I *know* your cousin. (b) *INCORRECT:* I ~~am knowing~~ your cousin.	Some verbs, like **know**, are *non-progressive;* * i.e., they are rarely used in progressive tenses. They describe states, not actions. ("States" are conditions or situations that exist.)

Common Verbs That Are Usually Non-Progressive (like *know*)

know	like	dislike	belong	consist of	hear	agree
believe	appreciate	fear	possess	contain	sound	disagree
doubt	care about	hate	own			mean
recognize	please	mind		exist	seem	promise
remember	prefer		desire	matter	look like	amaze
suppose			need		resemble	surprise
understand			want			
			wish			

(c) I *think* that your cousin is very nice. (d) I *'m thinking* about my trip to Rome.	Some verbs, like **think**, have both *non-progressive* meanings and *progressive* meanings. In (c): **think** means "believe." In (d): **am thinking** means "thoughts are going around in my mind right now."

Common Verbs with Both Non-Progressive and Progressive Meanings (like *think*)

	NON-PROGRESSIVE	PROGRESSIVE
look appear think feel have see taste smell love be	It *looks* cold outside. Jack *appears* to be tired today. I *think* that Mr. Liu is a good teacher. I *feel* that Mr. Liu is a good teacher. I *have* a bicycle. *Do* you *see* that bird? The soup *tastes* salty. Something *smells* bad. What is it? Ken *loves* his baby daughter. Mary *is* old and wise.	Olga *is looking* out the window. She*'s appearing* on a TV show today. I *'m thinking* about my family right now. I *'m feeling* a little tired today. I *'m having* a good time. The doctor *is seeing* a patient right now. The chef *is tasting* the soup. Ann *is smelling* the perfume to see if she wants to buy it. Ken is enjoying parenthood. In fact, he*'s loving* it! Al is ill but won't see a doctor. He *is being foolish.***

*Non-progressive verbs are also called "stative verbs" or non-action verbs.

Am/is/are being + an adjective describes temporary behavior. In the example, Al is usually not foolish, but right now he is acting that way.

2-4 Regular and Irregular Verbs

Regular Verbs: The simple past and past participle end in -ed.

SIMPLE FORM	SIMPLE PAST	PAST PARTICIPLE	PRESENT PARTICIPLE
hope	hoped	hoped	hoping
stop	stopped	stopped	stopping
listen	listened	listened	listening
study	studied	studied	studying
start	started	started	starting

English verbs have four principal parts:
(1) simple form
(2) simple past
(3) past participle
(4) present participle

Irregular Verbs: The simple past and past participle do not end in -ed.

SIMPLE FORM	SIMPLE PAST	PAST PARTICIPLE	PRESENT PARTICIPLE
hit	hit	hit	hitting
find	found	found	finding
swim	swam	swum	swimming
break	broke	broken	breaking

Some verbs have irregular past forms.

Most of the irregular verbs in English are given in the alphabetical list on the inside front and back covers.

Sarah *found* the correct chemical formula and *started* a new experiment.

2-5 Irregular Verb List

Group 1: All three forms are the same.

SIMPLE FORM	SIMPLE PAST	PAST PARTICIPLE	SIMPLE FORM	SIMPLE PAST	PAST PARTICIPLE
bet	bet	bet	let	let	let
burst	burst	burst	put	put	put
cost	cost	cost	quit	quit	quit
cut	cut	cut	shut	shut	shut
fit	fit/fitted	fit/fitted	split	split	split
hit	hit	hit	spread	spread	spread
hurt	hurt	hurt	upset	upset	upset

Group 2: Past participle ends in *-en*.

awake	awoke	awoken	hide	hid	hidden
bite	bit	bitten	prove	proved	proven/proved
break	broke	broken	ride	rode	ridden
choose	chose	chosen	rise	rose	risen
drive	drove	driven	shake	shook	shaken
eat	ate	eaten	speak	spoke	spoken
fall	fell	fallen	steal	stole	stolen
forget	forgot	forgotten	swell	swelled	swollen/swelled
forgive	forgave	forgiven	take	took	taken
freeze	froze	frozen	wake	woke/waked	woken
get	got	gotten/got*	write	wrote	written
give	gave	given			

* In BrE: *get-got-got*.

Group 3: Vowel changes from *a* in the simple past to *u* in the past participle.

begin	began	begun	shrink	shrank	shrunk
drink	drank	drunk	sing	sang	sung
ring	rang	rung	sink	sank	sunk
run	ran	run	swim	swam	swum

The chef **put** too much salt in the sauce.
He **had forgotten** the recipe.

Group 4: Past tense and past participle forms are the same.

bend	bent	bent	mislay	mislaid	mislaid
bleed	bled	bled	pay	paid	paid
bring	brought	brought	read	read	read
build	built	built	say	said	said
burn	burnt	burnt	seek	sought	sought
buy	bought	bought	sell	sold	sold
catch	caught	caught	send	sent	sent
dig	dug	dug	shoot	shot	shot
feed	fed	fed	sit	sat	sat
feel	felt	felt	sleep	slept	slept
fight	fought	fought	slide	slid	slid
find	found	found	sneak	snuck/sneaked	snuck/sneaked
flee	fled	fled	speed	sped/speeded	sped/speeded
grind	ground	ground	spend	spent	spent
hang	hung	hung	spin	spun	spun
have	had	had	stand	stood	stood
hear	heard	heard	stick	stuck	stuck
hold	held	held	sting	stung	stung
keep	kept	kept	strike	struck	struck
lay	laid	laid	sweep	swept	swept
lead	led	led	swing	swung	swung
leave	left	left	teach	taught	taught
lend	lent	lent	tell	told	told
light	lit/lighted	lit/lighted	think	thought	thought
lose	lost	lost	understand	understood	understood
make	made	made	weep	wept	wept
mean	meant	meant	win	won	won
meet	met	met			

Group 5: Past participle adds -*n* to the simple form, with or without a spelling change.

blow	blew	blown	see	saw	seen
do	did	done	swear	swore	sworn
draw	drew	drawn	tear	tore	torn
fly	flew	flown	throw	threw	thrown
grow	grew	grown	wear	wore	worn
know	knew	known	withdraw	withdrew	withdrawn
lie	lay	lain			

Group 6: The first and third forms are the same.

become	became	become
come	came	come
run	ran	run

Group 7: One of the three forms is very different.

be	was, were	been
go	went	gone

Group 8: Both regular and irregular forms are used. (The regular form is more common in AmE, and the irregular form is more common in BrE.)

burn	burned/burnt	burned/burnt	learn	learned/learnt	learned/learnt
dream	dreamed/dreamt	dreamed/dreamt	smell	smelled/smelt	smelled/smelt
kneel	kneeled/knelt	kneeled/knelt	spill	spilled/spilt	spilled/spilt
lean	leaned/leant	leaned/leant	spoil	spoiled/spoilt	spoiled/spoilt

NOTE: See the inside front and back covers for an alphabetical list of these verbs as well as some additional irregular verbs that occur less frequently. Also included are definitions of the lesser-known verbs.

2-6 Regular Verbs: Pronunciation of *-ed* Endings

Final **-ed** has three different pronunciations: /t/, /d/, and /əd/. The schwa /ə/ is an unstressed vowel sound. It is pronounced like *a* in *alone* in normal, rapid speech (e.g., *She lives alone.*).

(a) looked → look/t/ clapped → clap/t/ missed → miss/t/ watched → watch/t/ finished → finish/t/ laughed → laugh/t/	Final **-ed** is pronounced /t/ after voiceless sounds. Voiceless sounds are made by pushing air through your mouth; no sound comes from your throat. Examples of voiceless sounds: "k," "p," "s," "ch," "sh," "f."
(b) smelled → smell/d/ saved → save/d/ cleaned → clean/d/ robbed → rob/d/ played → play/d/	Final **-ed** is pronounced /d/ after voiced sounds. Voiced sounds come from your throat. If you touch your neck when you make a voiced sound, you can feel your voice box vibrate. Examples of voiced sounds: "l," "v," "n," "b," and all vowel sounds.

(c) decided → decide/əd/
needed → need/əd/
wanted → want/əd/
invited → invite/əd/
	Final **-ed** is pronounced /əd/ after "t" and "d" sounds. The sound /əd/ adds a whole syllable to a word.
	COMPARE: looked = one syllable → look/t/
	                smelled = one syllable → smell/d/
	                needed = two syllables → need/əd/

She **mopped** the kitchen floor,
vacuumed the carpet, and
dusted the furniture.

2-7 Simple Past

	(a) I **walked** to school yesterday. (b) John **lived** in Paris for ten years, but now he lives in Rome. (c) I **bought** a new car three days ago.	The simple past indicates that an activity or situation *began and ended at a particular time in the past.*
	(d) Rita **stood** under a tree *when it began to rain.* (e) *When Mrs. Chu **heard** a strange noise,* she **got** up to investigate. (f) *When I **dropped** my cup,* the coffee **spilled** on my lap.	If a sentence contains **when** and has the simple past in both clauses, the action in the *when*-clause happens first. In (d): 1st: The rain began. 2nd: Rita stood under a tree.

2-8 Past Progressive

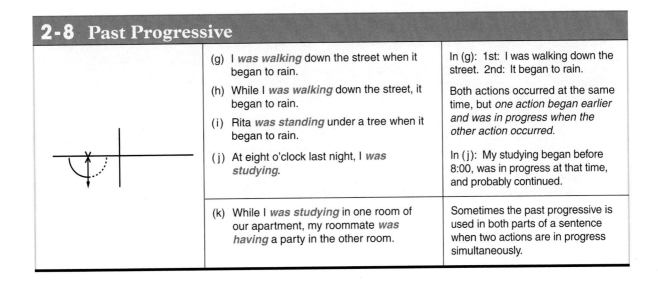

(g) I *was walking* down the street when it began to rain.	In (g): 1st: I was walking down the street. 2nd: It began to rain.
(h) While I *was walking* down the street, it began to rain.	Both actions occurred at the same time, but *one action began earlier and was in progress when the other action occurred.*
(i) Rita *was standing* under a tree when it began to rain.	
(j) At eight o'clock last night, I *was studying*.	In (j): My studying began before 8:00, was in progress at that time, and probably continued.
(k) While I *was studying* in one room of our apartment, my roommate *was having* a party in the other room.	Sometimes the past progressive is used in both parts of a sentence when two actions are in progress simultaneously.

2-9 Using Progressive Verbs with *Always*

(a) Mary *always leaves* for school at 7:45.	In sentences referring to present time, usually the simple present is used with *always* to describe habitual or everyday activities, as in (a).
(b) Mary *is always leaving* her dirty socks on the floor for me to pick up! Who does she think I am? Her maid?	In special circumstances, a speaker may use the present progressive with *always* to express annoyance, as in (b).
(c) I am *always/forever/constantly picking* up Mary's dirty socks!	In addition to *always*, the words *forever* and *constantly* are used with progressive verbs to express annoyance.

2-10 Using Expressions of Place with Progressive Verbs

(a) — What is Kay doing? — She*'s studying in her room*.	In usual word order, an expression of place follows a verb. In (a): *is studying* + *in her room* = the focus is on Kay's activity.
(b) — Where's Kay? — She*'s in her room studying*.	An expression of place can sometimes come between the auxiliary *be* and the *-ing* verb in a progressive verb form. In (b): *was* + *in her room* + *studying* = the focus is on Kay's location.

Chapter 3
Perfect and Perfect Progressive Tenses

3-1 Present Perfect

(a) 2002 — now / up to now	(a) Mrs. Oh *has been* a teacher *since* 2002. (b) I *have been* in this city *since* last May. (c) We *have been* here *since* nine o'clock.	The present perfect is often used with *since* and *for* to talk about *situations that began in the past and continue up to now.* In (a): SITUATION = being a teacher TIME FRAME = from 2002 up to now
	(d) Rita knows Rob. They met two months ago. She *has known* him *for* two months. I met him three years ago. I *have known* him *for* three years. (e) I *have known* Rob *since* I was in high school.	Notice the use of *since* vs. *for* in the examples: **since** + *a specific point in time* (e.g., *2002, last May, nine o'clock*) **for** + *a length of time* (e.g., *two months, three years*) In (e): **since** + *a time clause* (i.e., a subject and verb may follow *since*).*
(f) time? — now	(f) — *Have* you *ever seen* snow? — No, I *haven't*. I*'ve never seen* snow. But Anna has *seen* snow. (g) *Have* you *finished* your homework *yet*? I *still haven't finished* mine. Jack *has already finished* his.	The present perfect can talk about *events that have (or haven't) happened before now.* The exact time of the event is unspecified. The adverbs *ever, never, yet, still,* and *already* are often used with the present perfect. In (f): EVENT = seeing snow TIME FRAME = from the beginning of their lives up to now In (g): EVENT = doing homework TIME FRAME = from the time the people started up to now
(h) beginning of term — now / up to now / test 1 test 2 test 3	(h) We *have had* three tests *so far* this term. (i) I*'ve met* many people *since* I came here.	The present perfect can also express *an event that has occurred repeatedly from a point in the past up to the present time.* The event may happen again. In (h): REPEATED EVENT = taking tests TIME FRAME = from the beginning of the term up to now In (i): REPEATED EVENT = meeting people TIME FRAME = from the time I came here up to now
CONTRACTIONS: (j) *I've* been there. *You've* been there. *We've* been there. *They've* been there. *He's* been there. *She's* been there. *It's* been interesting.		**Have** and **has** are usually contracted with personal pronouns in informal writing, as in (j). NOTE: **He's** there. **He's** = *He is* **He's** been there. **He's** = *He has*

*See Chart 18-2, p. 96, for more information about time clauses.

3-2 *Have* and *Has* in Spoken English

(a) **How have** you been?
 	
    Spoken: How/v/ you been? OR
                 How/əv/ you been?
 	
(b) **Jane has** already eaten lunch.
 	
    Spoken: Jane/z/ already eaten lunch. OR
                 Jane/əz/ already eaten lunch.
 	
(c) **Mike has** already left.
 	
    Spoken: Mike/s/ already left. OR
                 Mike/əs/ already left.
	In spoken English, the present perfect helping verbs **has** and **have** are often reduced following nouns and question words.*
	
	In (a): **have** can sound like /v/ or /əv/.
	
	In (b): **has** can sound like /z/ or /əz/.
	
	In (c): **has** can sound like /s/ or /əs/.**
	
	--- 	
	
	NOTE: Jane/z/ eaten. **Jane's** = **Jane has**
	        Jane/z/ here. **Jane's** = **Jane is**
	
	        Mike/s/ left. **Mike's** = **Mike has**
	        Mike/s/ here. **Mike's** = **Mike is**

*In very informal writing, **has** is sometimes contracted with nouns (e.g., **Jane's** *already eaten.*) and question words (e.g., **Where's** *he gone?*). **Have** is rarely contracted in writing except with pronouns (e.g., *I've*). See Chart 3-1 for written contractions of **have** and **has** with pronouns. See Appendix Chart C for more information about contractions in general.

**See Chart 6-1, p. 25, for the pronunciation of final *-s* after voiced and voiceless sounds.

Written: **Paul has** started too many projects. **He has** decided to rest for a while.

Spoken: Paul /z/ (OR Paul/əz/) started too many projects.

         He /z/ decided to rest for a while.

Present Perfect vs. Simple Past

Present Perfect	(a) I **'ve met** Linda, but I **haven't met** her husband. **Have** you **met** them?	The PRESENT PERFECT is used to talk about *past events when there is no specific mention of time.* In (a): The speaker is talking about *some unspecified time before now.*
Simple Past	(b) I **met** Helen *yesterday* at a party. Her husband **was** there too, but I **didn't meet** him. **Did** you **meet** them at the party?	The SIMPLE PAST is used when there is *a specific mention of time.* In (b): The speaker is thinking of a specific time: yesterday.
Present Perfect	(c) Sam **has been** a teacher *for* ten years. He loves teaching.	The PRESENT PERFECT is used for *situations that began in the past and continue to the present.* In (c): The present perfect tells us that Sam is still a teacher now.
Simple Past	(d) Jim **was** a teacher *for* ten years, from 1995 to 2005. Now he is a salesman.	The SIMPLE PAST is used for *situations that began and ended in the past.* In (d): The simple past tells us that Jim is not a teacher now.

I've heard a lot of good things about Professor Stevens, but I haven't taken any of her classes. Have you?

Yes. I took one of her classes last year. I loved it.

3-4 Present Perfect Progressive

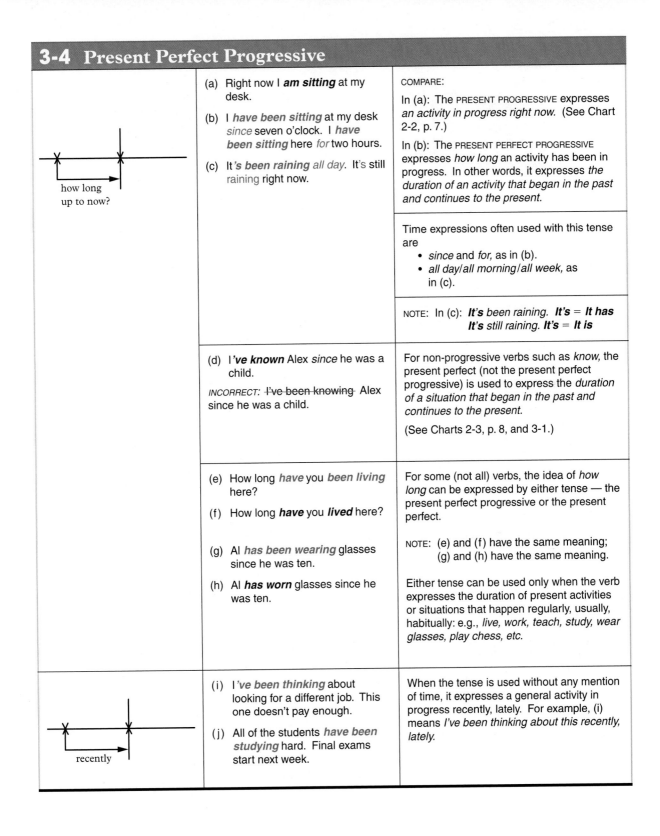

how long up to now?	(a) Right now I **am sitting** at my desk. (b) I **have been sitting** at my desk *since* seven o'clock. I **have been sitting** here *for* two hours. (c) It **'s been raining** *all day*. It's still raining right now.	COMPARE: In (a): The PRESENT PROGRESSIVE expresses *an activity in progress right now.* (See Chart 2-2, p. 7.) In (b): The PRESENT PERFECT PROGRESSIVE expresses *how long* an activity has been in progress. In other words, it expresses *the duration of an activity that began in the past and continues to the present.*
		Time expressions often used with this tense are • *since* and *for,* as in (b). • *all day/all morning/all week,* as in (c).
		NOTE: In (c): **It's** *been raining.* **It's** = **It has** **It's** *still raining.* **It's** = **It is**
	(d) I **'ve known** Alex *since* he was a child. INCORRECT: ~~I've been knowing~~ Alex since he was a child.	For non-progressive verbs such as *know,* the present perfect (not the present perfect progressive) is used to express the *duration of a situation that began in the past and continues to the present.* (See Charts 2-3, p. 8, and 3-1.)
	(e) How long *have* you **been living** here? (f) How long **have** you **lived** here? (g) Al **has been wearing** glasses since he was ten. (h) Al **has worn** glasses since he was ten.	For some (not all) verbs, the idea of *how long* can be expressed by either tense — the present perfect progressive or the present perfect. NOTE: (e) and (f) have the same meaning; (g) and (h) have the same meaning. Either tense can be used only when the verb expresses the duration of present activities or situations that happen regularly, usually, habitually: e.g., *live, work, teach, study, wear glasses, play chess,* etc.
recently	(i) I **'ve been thinking** about looking for a different job. This one doesn't pay enough. (j) All of the students **have been studying** hard. Final exams start next week.	When the tense is used without any mention of time, it expresses a general activity in progress recently, lately. For example, (i) means *I've been thinking about this recently, lately.*

3-5 Past Perfect

	(a) Sam arrived at 10:00. Ann left at 9:30. In other words, Ann *had* already *left* when Sam arrived.	The past perfect expresses *an activity that was complete before another activity or time in the past.*

(b) *By the time* Sam got there, Ann *had* already *left.*	In (a): 1st: Ann left. 2nd: Sam arrived. Adverb clauses with *by the time* are frequently used with the past perfect in the main clause, as in (b).*
(c) Sam *had left* before Ann got there. (d) Sam *left* before Ann got there. (e) *After* the guests *had left,* I went to bed. (f) *After* the guests *left,* I went to bed.	If either *before* or *after* is used in the sentence, the past perfect is often not necessary because the time relationship is already clear. The simple past may be used, as in (d) and (f). NOTE: (c) and (d) have the same meaning; (e) and (f) have the same meaning.
(g) *Actual spoken words:* I *lost* my keys. (h) *Reported words:* Jenny **said that** she *had lost* her keys.	The past perfect is commonly used in reported speech.** If the actual spoken words use the simple past, the past perfect is often used in reporting those words, as in (h). Common reporting verbs include *tell (someone), say, find out, learn,* and *discover.*
(i) *Written:* Bill *felt* great that evening. Earlier in the day, Annie *had caught* one fish, and he *had caught* three. They *had had* a delicious picnic near the lake and then *had gone* swimming again. It *had been* a nearly perfect vacation day.	The past perfect is often found in more formal writing such as fiction. In (i), the fiction writer uses the simple past to say that an event happened (*Bill felt great*), and then uses the past perfect to explain what had happened before that event.
(j) *I'd* finished. *You'd* finished. *We'd* finished. *They'd* finished. *She'd* finished. *He'd* finished. *It'd* finished.	***Had*** is often contracted with personal pronouns in informal writing. NOTE: *I'd* finished. *I'd = I had* *I'd* like to go. *I'd = I would*

*For more information about *by the time,* see Chart 17-2, p. 91.

**For more information about verb form usage in reported speech, see Chart 12-7, p. 67.

3-6 *Had* in Spoken English

(a) ***Joe had*** already heard the story.
    Spoken: Joe/d/ already heard the story. OR
                  Joe/əd/ already heard the story.
 	
(b) ***Who had*** been there before you?
    Spoken: Who/d/ been there before you? OR
                  Who/əd/ been there before you?
	In spoken English, the helping verb ***had*** in the past perfect is often reduced following nouns and question words. It can be pronounced as /d/ or as /əd/.*

(c) The dog ***had*** a bone. *Spoken:* The dog ***had*** a bone.	***Had*** is not reduced when it is a main verb, as in (c).

*See Chart 3-5 for written contractions of ***had*** with pronouns.

3-7 Past Perfect Progressive

4:30 6:00 ✗——✗ ⌐_____→ duration of waiting	(a) Eric finally came at six o'clock. I ***had been waiting*** for him *since* four-thirty. (b) The police ***had been looking*** for the criminal *for* two years before they caught him.	The past perfect progressive emphasizes the *duration of an activity that was in progress before another activity or time in the past.* NOTE: The past perfect progressive is used infrequently compared to other verb tenses.
✗✗ ⌐_→ close in time	(c) When Judy got home, her hair was still wet because she ***had been*** swimming. (d) I went to Ed's house after the funeral. His eyes were red because he ***had been crying***.	This tense also may express an activity *in progress close in time to another activity or time in the past.*
(e) *Actual spoken words:* I ***have been waiting*** for you. (f) *Reported words:* Lia ***told me that*** she ***had been waiting*** for me.		The past perfect progressive also occurs in reported speech. See Chart 3-5, examples (g) and (h).

Chapter 4
Future Time

<hr>

4-1 Simple Future: *Will* and *Be Going To*

(a) Jack *will* finish his work tomorrow. (b) Jack *is going to* finish his work tomorrow.	*Will* and *be going to* express future time and often have essentially the same meaning. Examples (a) and (b) have the same meaning. See Chart 4-2 for differences in meaning between the two forms.

Will

(c) Anna *will* come tomorrow around 5:00. *INCORRECT:* Anna ~~wills~~ come. *INCORRECT:* Anna ~~will~~ comes. *INCORRECT:* Anna ~~will~~ to come.	*Will* typically expresses predictions about the future, as in (c). *Will* does not take a final *-s*. *Will* is followed immediately by the simple form of a verb.
(d) Alex *will not be* here tomorrow. Peter *won't be* here either.	NEGATIVE: *will* + *not* = *won't*
(e) *Will* you *be* here tomorrow? How *will* you *get* here?	QUESTION: *will* + *subject* + *main verb* In (e): The speaker is asking for information about a future event.*
(f) *Spoken* or *written:* *I'll* be there. (g) *Spoken:* *Tom'll* be there too. *Written:* Tom will be there too. (h) *Spoken* or *very informal writing:* *Nobody'll* notice. *That'll* be fun. *There'll* be a test tomorrow.	CONTRACTIONS WITH PRONOUNS AND NOUNS: *Will* is often contracted with pronouns in both speaking and informal writing: *I'll, you'll, she'll, he'll, it'll, we'll, they'll.* *Will* is also often contracted with nouns in speaking but usually not in writing, as in (g). In very informal writing, *will* may be contracted with other kinds of pronouns and *there,* as in (h).

Be Going To

(i) Anna *is going to* come tomorrow around 5:00. (j) *Informally spoken:* Anna *'s gonna* come tomorrow around 5:00. (k) Tom *isn't going to* come. (l) *Are you going to* come?	*Be going to* also commonly expresses predictions about the future. In informal speech, *going to* is often pronounced "gonna." NEGATIVE: *be* + *not* + *going to*, as in (k) QUESTION: *be* + *subject* + *going to*, as in (l)

*****Will* can also be used in questions to make polite requests: ***Will*** *you* **open** *the door for me, please?* See Chart 9-3, p. 43.

4-2 *Will* vs. *Be Going To*

Prediction

(a) According to the weather report, it *will be* cloudy tomorrow. (b) According to the weather report, it *is going to be* cloudy tomorrow.	*Will* and *be going to* mean the same when they make *predictions* about the future (*prediction* = a statement about something the speaker thinks will be true or will occur in the future). Examples (a) and (b) have the same meaning.

Prior Plan

(c) —Why did you buy this paint? —I*'m going to paint* my bedroom tomorrow.	*Be going to* (but not *will*) is used to express a *prior plan* (i.e., a plan made before the moment of speaking).* In (c): The speaker already has a plan to paint his/her bedroom.

Willingness

(d) —The phone's ringing.
    —I*'ll get* it.
 	
(e) —How old is Aunt Agnes?
    —I don't know. She *won't tell* me.
 	
(f) The car *won't start*. Maybe the battery is dead.
	Will (but not *be going to*) is used to express *willingness*. In this case, *will* expresses a decision the speaker makes at the moment of speaking.
	
	In (d): The speaker decides to answer the phone at the immediate present moment; she/he does not have a prior plan.
	
	Will not / *won't* can express *refusal*, as in (e) with a person or in (f) with an inanimate object.

*Compare:
Situation 1: A: *Are you busy this evening?*
          B: *Yes.* ***I'm going to meet*** *Jack at the library at seven. We****'re going to study*** *together.*
In Situation 1, only ***be going to*** is possible. The speaker has a prior plan, so he uses ***be going to***.

Situation 2: A: *Are you busy this evening?*
          B: *Well, I really haven't made any plans. I****'ll eat*** (OR ***I'm going to eat***) *dinner, of course. And then I****'ll probably watch*** (OR ***I'm probably going to watch***) *TV for a little while.*
In Situation 2, either ***will*** or ***be going to*** is possible. Speaker B has not planned his evening. He is "predicting" his evening (rather than stating any prior plans), so he may use either ***will*** or ***be going to***.

Cho has a bad cough.
It *will be* worse by tomorrow if she doesn't get help.
She*'s going to go* to a doctor today.
Her husband *will drive* her there.

4-3 Expressing the Future in Time Clauses

(a) Bob will come soon. *When Bob **comes**, we will see him.*	In (a): ***When Bob comes** is a time clause.* **when** + subject + verb = a time clause* When the meaning of the time clause is future, the SIMPLE PRESENT tense is used. *Will* or *be going to* is not used in the time clause.
(b) Linda is going to leave soon. *Before she **leaves**,* she is going to finish her work.	
(c) I will get home at 5:30. *After I **get** home,* I will eat dinner.	A time clause begins with such words as *when, before, after, as soon as, until,* and *while* and includes a subject and a verb. The time clause can come either at the beginning of the sentence or in the second part of the sentence: *When he comes,* we'll see him. OR We'll see him *when he comes.* Notice: A comma is used when the time clause comes first in a sentence.
(d) The taxi will arrive soon. *As soon as it **arrives**,* we'll be able to leave for the airport.	
(e) They are going to come soon. I'll wait here *until they **come**.*	
(f) *While I **am traveling** in Europe next year,* I'm going to save money by staying in youth hostels.	Sometimes the PRESENT PROGRESSIVE is used in a time clause to express an activity that will be in progress in the future, as in (f).
(g) I will go to bed *after I **finish** my work.*	Occasionally, the PRESENT PERFECT is used in a time clause, as in (h). Examples (g) and (h) have the same meaning. The present perfect in the time clause emphasizes the completion of one act before a second act occurs in the future.
(h) I will go to bed *after I **have finished** my work.*	

*A *time clause* is an adverb clause. See Charts 17-1 (p. 90) and 17-2 (p. 91) for more information.

4-4 Using the Present Progressive and the Simple Present to Express Future Time

Present Progressive

(a) My wife has an appointment with a doctor. She *is seeing* Dr. North *next Tuesday.*	The PRESENT PROGRESSIVE may be used to *express future time when the idea of the sentence concerns a planned event or definite intention.*
(b) Sam has already made his plans. He *is leaving* at noon tomorrow.	COMPARE: A verb such as *rain* is not used in the present progressive to indicate future time because rain is not a planned event.
(c) — What are you going to do this afternoon? — *After lunch,* I *am meeting* a friend of mine. We *are going* shopping. Would you like to come along?	A future meaning for the present progressive tense is indicated either by future time words in the sentence or by the context.

Simple Present

(d) The museum *opens* at 10:00 tomorrow morning.	The SIMPLE PRESENT can also be used to *express future time in a sentence concerning events that are on a definite schedule or timetable.* These sentences usually contain future time words. Only a few verbs are used in this way: e.g., *open, close, begin, end, start, finish, arrive, leave, come, return.*
(e) Classes *begin* next week.	
(f) John's plane *arrives* at 6:05 P.M. next Monday.	

4-5 Future Progressive

	(a) I will begin to study at seven. You will come at eight. I *will be studying* when you come.	The future progressive expresses an activity that *will be in progress at a time in the future.*
	(b) Don't call me at nine because I won't be home. I *am going to be studying* at the library.	The progressive form of *be going to:* **be going to** + **be** + **-ing**, as in (b)
	(c) Don't worry. She *will be coming* soon. (d) Don't worry. She *will come* soon.	Sometimes there is little or no difference between the future progressive and the simple future, especially when the future event will occur at an indefinite time in the future, as in (c) and (d).

4-6 Future Perfect and Future Perfect Progressive

NOTE: These two tenses are rarely used compared to the other verb tenses.

Future Perfect	(a) I will graduate in June. I will see you in July. By the time I see you, I *will have graduated.*	The FUTURE PERFECT expresses an activity that will be *completed before another time or event in the future.*
Future Perfect Progressive	(b) I will go to bed at 10:00 P.M. Ed will get home at midnight. At midnight I will be sleeping. I *will have been sleeping* for two hours by the time Ed gets home.	The FUTURE PERFECT PROGRESSIVE emphasizes the *duration* of an activity that will be *in progress before another time or event in the future.*
	(c) When Professor Jones retires next month, he *will have taught* OR *will have been teaching* for 45 years.	Sometimes the future perfect and the future perfect progressive have the same meaning, as in (c). Also, notice that the activity expressed by either of these two tenses may begin in the past.

Chapter 5
Review of Verb Tenses

LISA: Why are there no charts in Chapter 5?
BOB: Because it's a review chapter.

Chapter 6
Subject-Verb Agreement

6-1 Final -s/-es: Use, Pronunciation, and Spelling

Use

(a) *Noun + -s:* *Friends* are important. *Noun + -es:* I like my *classes*.	A final *-s* or *-es* is added to a noun to make the noun plural. **Friend** and **class** = singular nouns **Friends** and **classes** = plural nouns
(b) *Verb + -s:* Mary *works* at the bank. *Verb + -es:* John *watches* birds.	A final *-s* or *-es* is added to a simple present verb when the subject is a singular noun (e.g., *Mary, my father, the machine*) or third person singular pronoun (*she, he, it*). **Mary works** = singular **She works** = singular **The students work** = plural **They work** = plural

Pronunciation

(c)	seats ropes backs	→ seat/s/ → rope/s/ → back/s/	Final *-s* is pronounced /s/ after voiceless sounds, as in (c): "t," "p," and "k" are examples of voiceless sounds.*
(d)	seeds robes bags sees	→ seed/z/ → robe/z/ → bag/z/ → see/z/	Final *-s* is pronounced /z/ after voiced sounds, as in (d): "d," "b," "g," and "ee" are examples of voiced sounds.*
(e)	dishes catches kisses mixes prizes edges	→ dish/əz/ → catch/əz/ → kiss/əz/ → mix/əz/ → prize/əz/ → edge/əz/	Final *-s* and *-es* are pronounced /əz/ after "sh," "ch," "s," "x," "z," and "ge"/"dge" sounds. The /əz/ ending adds a syllable. All of the words in (e) are pronounced with two syllables. COMPARE: All of the words in (c) and (d) are pronounced with one syllable.

Spelling

(f)	sing song	→ sings → songs	For most words (whether a verb or a noun), simply add a final *-s* to spell the word correctly.
(g)	wash watch class buzz box	→ washes → watches → classes → buzzes → boxes	Final *-es* is added to words that end in *-sh, -ch, -s, -z,* and *-x.*

(h)
 	
(i)
	toy
	buy
	baby
	cry
		→ toys
		→ buys
		→ babies
		→ cries
			For words that end in *-y:*
			   In (h): If *-y* is preceded by a vowel, only *-s* is added.
			   In (i): If *-y* is preceded by a consonant, the *-y* is changed to *-i* and *-es* is added.

*See Chart 2-6, p. 12, for an explanation of voiced vs. voiceless sounds.

6-2 Basic Subject-Verb Agreement

Singular Verb	Plural Verb	
(a) My *friend* **lives** in Boston.	(b) My *friends* **live** in Boston.	*Verb* + **-s/-es** = third person singular in the simple present tense *Noun* + **-s/-es** = plural
	(c) My *brother* **and** *sister* **live** in Boston. (d) My *brother, sister,* **and** *cousin* **live** in Boston.	Two or more subjects connected by **and** require a plural verb.
(e) **Every** *man, woman,* **and** *child* **needs** love. (f) **Each** *book* **and** *magazine* **is** listed in the bibliography.		EXCEPTION: **Every** and **each** are always followed immediately by singular nouns. (See Chart 7-11, p. 36.) In this case, even when there are two (or more) nouns connected by **and**, the verb is singular.
(g) That *book* on political parties **is** interesting. (i) The *book* that I got from my parents **was** very interesting.	(h) The *ideas* in that book **are** interesting. (j) The *books* I bought at the bookstore **were** expensive.	Sometimes a phrase or clause separates a subject from its verb. These interrupting structures do not affect basic agreement. For example, in (g) the interrupting prepositional phrase **on political parties** does not change the fact that the verb **is** must agree with the subject **book**. In (i) and (j): The subject and verb are separated by an adjective clause. (See Chapter 13.)
(k) *Watching* old movies **is** fun.		A gerund (e.g., *watching*) used as the subject of the sentence requires a singular verb. (See Chart 14-8, p. 81.)

The *bag* of groceries **was** too heavy
for Sonya to carry.

6-3 Subject-Verb Agreement: Using Expressions of Quantity

Singular Verb	Plural Verb	

(a) *Some of the* **book is** good.
(c) *A lot of the* **equipment is** new.
(e) *Two-thirds of the* **money is** mine.
(g) *Most of our* **homework is** easy.
	(b) *Some of the* **books are** good.
	(d) *A lot of my* **friends are** here.
	(f) *Two-thirds of the* **boys are** here.
	(h) *Most of our* **assignments are** easy.
		In most expressions of quantity, the verb is determined by the noun (or pronoun) that follows *of*.
		For example, in (a) and (b):
		    some of + singular noun = singular verb
		    some of + plural noun = plural verb

(i) **One** *of my friends* **is** here. (j) **Each** *of my friends* **is** here. (k) **Every one** *of my friends* **is** here.		EXCEPTIONS: **One of**, **each of**, and **every one of** take singular verbs. *one of* *each of* } + plural noun = singular verb *every one of*
(l) **None** *of the boys* **is** here.	(m) **None** *of the boys* **are** here.	Subjects with **none of** used to be considered singular in very formal English, but plural verbs are often used in informal English and sometimes even in formal writing.
(n) **The number** *of students* in the class **is** fifteen.	(o) *A number of* **students were** late for class.	COMPARE: In (n): **The number** is the subject. In (o): **A number of** is an expression of quantity meaning "a lot of." It is followed by a plural noun and a plural verb.

6-4 Subject-Verb Agreement: Using *There + Be*

(a) **There is** *a fly* in the room. (b) **There are** *three windows* in this room.	**There + be** introduces the idea that something exists in a particular place. **There + be** + subject + expression of place* The subject follows **be** when **there** is used. In (a): The subject is *a fly.* (singular) In (b): The subject is *three windows.* (plural)
(c) *INFORMAL:* **There**'s *two sides* to every story.	In informal spoken English, some native speakers use a singular verb even when the subject is plural, as in (c). The use of this form is fairly frequent but is not generally considered to be grammatically correct.

*Sometimes the expression of place is omitted when the meaning is clear. For example, *There are seven continents.* The implied expression of place is clearly *in the world.*

6-5 Subject-Verb Agreement: Some Irregularities

Singular Verb

(a) *The United States* **is** big. (b) *The Philippines* **consists** of more than 7,000 islands. (c) *The United Nations* **has** its headquarters in New York City. (d) *Harrods* **is** a department store.	Sometimes a proper noun that ends in **-s** is singular. In the examples, if the noun is changed to a pronoun, the singular pronoun **it** is used (not the plural pronoun **they**) because the noun is singular. In (a): **The United States** = **it** (not **they**)
(e) The *news* **is** interesting.	**News** is singular.
(f) *Mathematics* **is** easy for her. *Physics* **is** easy for her too.	Fields of study that end in **-ics** require singular verbs.
(g) *Diabetes* **is** an illness.	Certain illnesses that end in **-s** are singular: *diabetes, measles, mumps, rabies, rickets, shingles.*
(h) *Eight hours* of sleep **is** enough. (i) *Ten dollars* **is** too much to pay. (j) *Five thousand miles* **is** too far to travel.	Expressions of time, money, and distance usually require a singular verb.

(k) *Two and two* **is** four.
     Two and two **equals** four.
     Two plus two **is**/**equals** four.
 (l) *Five times five* **is** twenty-five.
	Arithmetic expressions require singular verbs.

Plural Verb

(m) *Those people* **are** from Canada. (n) *The police* **have** been called. (o) *Cattle* **are** domestic animals. (p) *Fish* **live** under water.	*People,* police, cattle,* and *fish* do not end in **-s**, but they are plural nouns in the example sentences and require plural verbs.

Singular Verb	Plural Verb	
(q) *English* **is** spoken in many countries. (s) *Chinese* **is** his native language.	(r) *The English* **drink** tea. (t) *The Chinese* **have** an interesting history.	In (q): **English** = language In (r): **The English** = people from England Some nouns of nationality that end in **-sh**, **-ese**, and **-ch** can mean either language or people, e.g., *English, Spanish, Chinese, Japanese, Vietnamese, Portuguese, French.*
	(u) *The poor* **have** many problems. (v) *The rich* **get** richer.	A few adjectives can be preceded by **the** and used as a plural noun (without final **-s**) to refer to people who have that quality. Other examples: *the young, the elderly, the living, the dead, the blind, the deaf, the disabled.*

*The word *people* has a final **-s** (*peoples*) only when it is used to refer to ethnic or national groups: *All the **peoples** of the world desire peace.*

Chapter 7
Nouns

7-1 Regular and Irregular Plural Nouns

(a) song—*songs*	The plural of most nouns is formed by adding final **-s**.*
(b) box—*boxes*	Final **-es** is added to nouns that end in **-sh**, **-ch**, **-s**, **-z**, and **-x**.*
(c) baby—*babies*	The plural of words that end in a consonant + **-y** is spelled **-ies**.*
(d) man—*men* ox—*oxen* tooth—*teeth* woman—*women* foot—*feet* mouse—*mice* child—*children* goose—*geese* louse—*lice*	The nouns in (d) have irregular plural forms that do not end in **-s**.
(e) echo—*echoes* potato—*potatoes* hero—*heroes* tomato—*tomatoes*	Some nouns that end in **-o** add **-es** to form the plural.
(f) auto—*autos* photo—*photos* studio—*studios* ghetto—*ghettos* piano—*pianos* tatoo—*tatoos* kangaroo—*kangaroos* radio—*radios* video—*videos* kilo—*kilos* solo—*solos* zoo—*zoos* memo—*memos* soprano—*sopranos*	Some nouns that end in **-o** add only **-s** to form the plural. NOTE: When in doubt, use your dictionary or spellcheck.
(g) memento—*mementoes/mementos* volcano—*volcanoes/volcanos* mosquito—*mosquitoes/mosquitos* zero—*zeroes/zeros* tornado—*tornadoes/tornados*	Some nouns that end in **-o** add either **-es** or **-s** to form the plural (with **-es** being the more usual plural form).
(h) calf—*calves* life—*lives* thief—*thieves* half—*halves* loaf—*loaves* wolf—*wolves* knife—*knives* self—*selves* scarf—*scarves/scarfs* leaf—*leaves* shelf—*shelves*	Some nouns that end in **-f** or **-fe** are changed to **-ves** to form the plural.
(i) belief—*beliefs* cliff—*cliffs* chief—*chiefs* roof—*roofs*	Some nouns that end in **-f** simply add **-s** to form the plural.
(j) one deer—*two deer* one series—*two series* one fish—*two fish*** one sheep—*two sheep* one means—*two means* one shrimp—*two shrimp**** one offspring—*two offspring* one species—*two species*	Some nouns have the same singular and plural form: e.g., *One deer is . . . .* *Two deer are . . . .*

(k) criterion—*criteria*   (m) analysis—*analyses*
     phenomenon—*phenomena*   basis—*bases*
                       crisis—*crises*
(l) bacterium—*bacteria*   hypothesis—*hypotheses*
     curriculum—*curricula*   parenthesis—*parentheses*
     datum—*data*   thesis—*theses*
     medium—*media*
     memorandum—*memoranda*
	Some nouns that English has borrowed from other languages have foreign plurals.

*For information about the pronunciation and spelling of words ending in *-s/-es,* see Chart 6-1, p. 25.

**Fishes is also possible but rarely used.

***Especially in British English, but also occasionally in American English, the plural of *shrimp* can be *shrimps*.

7-2 Possessive Nouns

Singular Noun	Possessive Form	To show possession, add an apostrophe (') and **-s** to a singular noun: *The **girl's** book is on the table.*
(a) the girl	*the girl's*	
(b) Tom	*Tom's*	If a singular noun ends in **-s**, there are two possible forms:
(c) my wife	*my wife's*	1. Add an apostrophe and **-s**: ***Thomas's*** *book.*
(d) a lady	*a lady's*	2. Add only an apostrophe: ***Thomas'*** *book.*
(e) Thomas	*Thomas's/Thomas'*	

Plural Noun	Possessive Form	Add only an apostrophe to a plural noun that ends in **-s**: *The **girls'** books are on the table.*
(f) the girls	*the girls'*	
(g) their wives	*their wives'*	Add an apostrophe and **-s** to plural nouns that do not end in **-s**: *The **men's** books are on the table.*
(h) the ladies	*the ladies'*	
(i) the men	*the men's*	
(j) my children	*my children's*	

(k) ***Alan and Lisa's*** apartment is on the third floor.	When two (or more) names are connected by **and**, only the final name shows possession.

7-3 Nouns as Adjectives

	When a noun is used as an adjective, it is in its singular form.*
The soup has vegetables in it.	
(a) It is ***vegetable*** soup.	*INCORRECT:* vegetable ~~-s~~ soup
The building has offices in it.	
(b) It is an ***office*** building.	

	When a noun used as a modifier is combined with a number expression, the noun is singular and a hyphen (-) is used.
The test lasted two hours.	
(c) It was a ***two-hour*** test.	*INCORRECT:* She has a five year ~~-s~~ old son.
Her son is five years old.	
(d) She has a ***five-year-old*** son.	

*Adjectives never take a final **-s** (*INCORRECT:* beautiful ~~-s~~ pictures). See Appendix Chart A-2.

Harry's bed has a ***mosquito*** net.

7-4 Count and Noncount Nouns

(a) I bought *a chair*. Sam bought *three chairs*.

(b) We bought *some furniture*.
   INCORRECT: We bought some furniture ~~s~~.
   INCORRECT: We bought ~~a~~ furniture.

Chair is called a "count noun." This means you can count chairs: *one chair, two chairs, etc.*

Furniture is called a "noncount noun." In grammar, you cannot use numbers (*one, two, etc.*) with the word **furniture**.

	Singular	**Plural**	
Count Noun	*a* chair *one* chair	*two* chairs *some* chairs *a lot of* chairs *many* chairs Ø chairs★	A count noun: (1) may be preceded by *a/an* or *one* in the singular. (2) takes a final *-s/-es* in the plural.
Noncount Noun	*some* furniture *a lot of* furniture *much* furniture Ø furniture★		A noncount noun: (1) is not immediately preceded by *a/an* or *one*. (2) has no plural form, so does not add a final *-s/-es*.

★Ø = nothing (i.e., no article or other determiner).

7-5 Noncount Nouns

(a) I bought some chairs, tables, and desks. In other words, I bought some *furniture*.	Many noncount nouns refer to a "whole" that is made up of different parts. In (a): *furniture* represents a whole group of things that is made up of similar but separate items.
(b) I put some *sugar* in my *coffee*.	In (b): *sugar* and *coffee* represent whole masses made up of individual particles or elements.★
(c) I wish you *luck*.	Many noncount nouns are abstractions. In (c): *luck* is an abstract concept, an abstract "whole." It has no physical form; you can't touch it; you can't count it.
(d) *Sunshine* is warm and cheerful.	A phenomenon of nature, such as *sunshine*, is frequently used as a noncount noun, as in (d).
(e) NONCOUNT: Ann has brown *hair*. COUNT: Tom has a *hair* on his jacket. (f) NONCOUNT: I opened the curtains to let in some *light*. COUNT: Don't forget to turn off the *light* before you go to bed.	Many nouns can be used as either noncount or count nouns, but the meaning is different, e.g., *hair* in (e) and *light* in (f). (Dictionaries written especially for learners of English as a second language are a good source of information on count/noncount usage of nouns.)

★To express a particular quantity, some noncount nouns may be preceded by unit expressions: *a spoonful of sugar, a glass of water, a cup of coffee, a quart of milk, a loaf of bread, a grain of rice, a bowl of soup, a bag of flour, a pound of meat, a piece of furniture, a piece of paper, a piece of jewelry.*

7-6 Some Common Noncount Nouns

This list is a sample of nouns that are commonly used as noncount nouns. Many other nouns can also be used as noncount nouns.

(a) WHOLE GROUPS MADE UP OF SIMILAR ITEMS: baggage, clothing, equipment, food, fruit, furniture, garbage, hardware, jewelry, junk, luggage, machinery, mail, makeup, money/cash/change, postage, scenery, stuff, traffic, etc.

(b) FLUIDS: water, coffee, tea, milk, oil, soup, gasoline, blood, etc.
(c) SOLIDS: ice, bread, butter, cheese, meat, gold, iron, silver, glass, paper, wood, cotton, wool, etc.
(d) GASES: steam, air, oxygen, nitrogen, smoke, smog, pollution, etc.
(e) PARTICLES: rice, chalk, corn, dirt, dust, flour, grass, hair, pepper, salt, sand, sugar, wheat, etc.

(f) ABSTRACTIONS:
—beauty, confidence, courage, education, enjoyment, fun, happiness, health, help, honesty, hospitality, importance, intelligence, justice, knowledge, laughter, luck, music, patience, peace, pride, progress, recreation, significance, sleep, truth, violence, wealth, etc.
—advice, information, news, evidence, proof, etc.
—time, space, energy, etc.
—homework, work, etc.
—grammar, slang, vocabulary, etc.
(g) LANGUAGES: Arabic, Chinese, English, Spanish, etc.
(h) FIELDS OF STUDY: chemistry, engineering, history, literature, mathematics, psychology, etc.
(i) RECREATION: baseball, soccer, tennis, chess, bridge, poker, etc.
(j) ACTIVITIES: driving, studying, swimming, traveling, walking (and other gerunds)

(k) NATURAL PHENOMENA: weather, dew, fog, hail, heat, humidity, lightning, rain, sleet, snow, thunder, wind, darkness, light, sunshine, electricity, fire, gravity, etc.

Gardening is Annie's favorite hobby.

7-7 Basic Article Usage

I. Using *A* or *Ø*: Generic Nouns

Singular Count Noun	(a) *A banana* is yellow.*	A speaker uses generic nouns to make generalizations. A generic noun represents a whole class of things; it is not a specific, real, concrete thing, but rather a symbol of a whole group.
Plural Count Noun	(b) *Ø Bananas* are yellow.	In (a) and (b): The speaker is talking about any banana, all bananas, bananas in general. In (c): The speaker is talking about any and all fruit, fruit in general.
Noncount Noun	(c) *Ø Fruit* is good for you.	Notice that no article (Ø) is used to make generalizations with plural count nouns, as in (b), and with noncount nouns, as in (c).

II. Using *A* or *Some:* Indefinite Nouns

Singular Count Noun	(d) I ate *a banana*.	Indefinite nouns are actual things (not symbols), but they are not specifically identified. In (d): The speaker is not referring to "this banana" or "that banana" or "the banana you gave me." The speaker is simply saying that she/he ate one banana. The listener does not know or need to know which specific banana was eaten; it was simply one banana out of all bananas.
Plural Count Noun	(e) I ate **some** *bananas*.	
Noncount Noun	(f) I ate **some** *fruit*.	In (e) and (f): **Some** is often used with indefinite plural count nouns and indefinite noncount nouns. In addition to **some**, a speaker might use *two, a few, several, a lot of, etc.*, with plural count nouns, or *a little, a lot of, etc.,* with noncount nouns. (See Chart 7-4.)

III. Using *The:* Definite Nouns

Singular Count Noun	(g) Thank you for *the banana*.	A noun is definite when both the speaker and the listener are thinking about the same specific thing.
Plural Count Noun	(h) Thank you for *the bananas*.	In (g): The speaker uses *the* because the listener knows which specific banana the speaker is talking about, i.e., that particular banana which the listener gave to the speaker. Notice that *the* is used with both singular and plural count nouns and with noncount nouns.
Noncount Noun	(i) Thank you for *the fruit*.	

*Usually *a/an* is used with a singular generic count noun. Examples: *A window is made of glass. A doctor heals sick people. Parents must give a child love. A box has six sides. An apple can be red, green, or yellow.*

   However, *the* is sometimes used with a singular generic count noun (not a plural generic count noun, not a generic noncount noun). "Generic *the*" is commonly used with, in particular:
   (1) species of animals: ***The blue whale** is the largest mammal on earth. **The elephant** is the largest land mammal.*
   (2) inventions: *Who invented **the telephone**? **the wheel**? **the refrigerator**? **the airplane**? **The computer** will play an increasingly large role in all of our lives.*
   (3) instruments: *I'd like to learn to play **the piano**. Do you play **the guitar**?*

7-8 General Guidelines for Article Usage

(a) **The sun** is bright today. Please hand this book to *the teacher*. Please open *the door*. Omar is in *the kitchen*.	GUIDELINE: Use **the** when you know or assume that your listener is familiar with and thinking about the same specific thing or person you are talking about.
(b) Yesterday I saw **some dogs**. *The dogs* were chasing *a cat*. *The cat* was chasing *a mouse*. *The mouse* ran into *a hole*. *The hole* was very small.	GUIDELINE: Use **the** for the second mention of an indefinite noun.* In (b): first mention = *some dogs, a cat, a mouse, a hole;* second mention = *the dogs, the cat, the mouse, the hole*
(c) CORRECT: **Apples** are my favorite fruit. INCORRECT: ~~The~~ apples are my favorite fruit. (d) CORRECT: **Gold** is a metal. INCORRECT: ~~The~~ gold is a metal.	GUIDELINE: Do NOT use **the** with a plural count noun (e.g., *apples*) or a noncount noun (e.g., *gold*) when you are making a generalization.
(e) CORRECT: (1) I drove *a car.* / I drove *the car*. (2) I drove *that car*. (3) I drove *his car*. INCORRECT: I drove car.	GUIDELINE: A singular count noun (e.g., *car*) is always preceded by: (1) an article (*a/an* or *the*); OR (2) *this/that*; OR (3) a possessive pronoun.

***The** is NOT used for the second mention of a generic noun. COMPARE:
(1) *What color is **a banana** (generic noun)? **A banana** (generic noun) is yellow.*
(2) *Joe offered me **a banana** (indefinite noun) or **an apple**. I chose **the banana** (definite noun).*

They have **a** rusty **car, some** broken **furniture,** and **an** old **refrigerator** in **the** front **yard**.

7-9 Expressions of Quantity Used with Count and Noncount Nouns

Expressions of Quantity	Used with Count Nouns	Used with Noncount Nouns	
(a) one each every	*one* apple *each* apple *every* apple	Ø* Ø Ø	An expression of quantity may precede a noun. Some expressions of quantity are used only with count nouns, as in (a) and (b).
(b) two, etc. both a couple of a few several many a number of	*two* apples *both* apples *a couple of* apples *a few* apples *several* apples *many* apples *a number of* apples	Ø Ø Ø Ø Ø Ø	
(c) a little much a great deal of	Ø Ø Ø	*a little* rice *much* rice *a great deal of* rice	Some are used only with noncount nouns, as in (c).
(d) no hardly any some/any a lot of/lots of plenty of most all	*no* apples *hardly any* apples *some*/*any* apples *a lot of*/*lots of* apples *plenty of* apples *most* apples *all* apples	*no* rice *hardly any* rice *some*/*any* rice *a lot of*/*lots of* rice *plenty of* rice *most* rice *all* rice	Some are used with both count and noncount nouns, as in (d).

*Ø = not used. For example, *one* is not used with noncount nouns. You can say "I ate one apple" but NOT "I ate one rice."

7-10 Using *A Few* and *Few*; *A Little* and *Little*

COUNT: (a) We sang *a few* songs. NONCOUNT: (b) We listened to *a little* music.	*A few* and *few* are used with plural count nouns, as in (a). *A little* and *little* are used with noncount nouns, as in (b).
(c) She has been here only two weeks, but she has already made *a few* friends. *(Positive idea: She has made some friends.)* (d) I'm very pleased. I've been able to save *a little* money this month. *(Positive idea: I have saved some money instead of spending all of it.)*	*A few* and *a little* give a positive idea; they indicate that something exists, is present, as in (c) and (d).
(e) I feel sorry for her. She has (*very*) *few* friends. *(Negative idea: She does not have many friends; she has almost no friends.)*	*Few* and *little* (without *a*) give a negative idea; they indicate that something is largely absent, as in (e). *Very* (+ *few*/*little*) makes the negative stronger, the number/amount smaller, as in (f).
(f) I have (*very*) *little* money. I don't even have enough money to buy food for dinner. *(Negative idea: I do not have much money; I have almost no money.)*	

7-11 Singular Expressions of Quantity: *One, Each, Every*

(a) *One student* was late to class. (b) *Each student* has a schedule. (c) *Every student* has a schedule.	*One*, *each*, and *every* are followed immediately by singular count nouns (never plural nouns, never noncount nouns).
(d) *One of the students* was late to class. (e) *Each (one) of the students* has a schedule (f) *Every one of the students* has a schedule.	*One of*, *each of*, and *every one of** are followed by specific plural count nouns (never singular nouns; never noncount nouns).

*COMPARE:

    Every one (two words) is an expression of quantity (e.g., *I have read **every one** of those books*).

    Everyone (one word) is an indefinite pronoun. It has the same meaning as *everybody* (e.g., ***Everyone/Everybody** has a schedule*).

NOTE: *Each* and *every* have essentially the same meaning.

    Each is used when the speaker is thinking of one person/thing at a time: ***Each** student has a schedule.* = *Mary has a schedule. Hiroshi has a schedule. Carlos has a schedule. Sabrina has a schedule. Etc.*

    Every is used when the speaker means *all*: ***Every** student has a schedule.* = ***All of** the students have schedules.*

7-12 Using *Of* in Expressions of Quantity

(a) I bought *one book*. (b) I bought *many books*.	With some expressions of quantity, *of* is not used when the noun is nonspecific, as in (a) and (b).
(c) *One of **those** books* is mine. (d) *Some of **the** books* are yours. (e) *Many of **my** books* are in Spanish. (f) *Most of **them*** are paperbacks.	*Of* is used with: • specific nouns, as in (c), (d), and (e). • pronouns, as in (f).
(g) I have *a lot of books*. (h) I've read *a lot of **those** books*.	Some expressions of quantity, like *a lot of*, always include *of*, whether the noun is nonspecific, as in (g), or specific, as in (h).

Expressions of quantity

one (of)	all (of)	some (of)
two (of)	each (of)	several (of)
half of	every	(a) few (of)
50 percent of	almost all (of)	(a) little (of)
three-fourths of	most (of)	hardly any (of)
a majority of	many (of)	none of
hundreds of	much (of)	no
thousands of	a number of	
millions of	a great deal of	
	a lot of	

Chapter 8
Pronouns

	Subject Pronoun	Object Pronoun	Possessive Pronoun	Possessive Adjective
Singular	*I* *you* *she, he, it*	*me* *you* *her, him, it*	*mine* *yours* *hers, his, its*	*my* (name) *your* (name) *her, his, its* (name)
Plural	*we* *you* *they*	*us* *you* *them*	*ours* *yours* *theirs*	*our* (names) *your* (names) *their* (names)

(a) I read *a book*. *It* was good.	A PRONOUN is used in place of a noun. The noun it refers to is called the "antecedent." In (a): The pronoun *it* refers to the antecedent noun *book*. A singular pronoun is used to refer to a singular noun, as in (a). A plural pronoun is used to refer to a plural noun, as in (b).
(b) I read *some books*. *They* were good.	
(c) *I* like tea. Do *you* like tea too?	Sometimes the antecedent noun is understood, not explicitly stated. In (c): *I* refers to the speaker, and *you* refers to the person the speaker is talking to.
(d) John has a car. *He drives* to work.	SUBJECT PRONOUNS are used as subjects of sentences, as *he* in (d).
(e) John works in my office. I *know him* well. (f) I talk *to him* every day.	OBJECT PRONOUNS are used as the objects of verbs, as *him* in (e), or as the objects of prepositions, as *him* in (f).
(g) That book is *hers*. *Yours* is over there. (h) *INCORRECT:* That book is ~~her's~~. ~~Your's~~ is over there.	POSSESSIVE PRONOUNS are not followed immediately by a noun; they stand alone, as in (g). Possessive pronouns DO NOT take apostrophes, as in (h). (See Chart 7-2, p. 30, for the use of apostrophes with possessive nouns.)
(i) *Her* book is here. *Your* book is over there.	POSSESSIVE ADJECTIVES are followed immediately by a noun; they do not stand alone.
(j) A bird uses *its* wings to fly. (k) *INCORRECT:* A bird uses ~~it's~~ wings to fly. (l) *It's* cold today. (m) The Harbour Inn is my favorite old hotel. *It's been* in business since 1933.	COMPARE: *Its* has NO APOSTROPHE when it is used as a possessive, as in (j). *It's* has an apostrophe when it is used as a contraction of *it is*, as in (l), or *it has* when *has* is part of the present perfect tense, as in (m). NOTE: *It's* VS. *its* is a common source of error for native speakers of English.

8-2 Personal Pronouns: Agreement with Generic Nouns and Indefinite Pronouns

(a) *A student* walked into the room. *She* was looking for the teacher.	In (a) and (b): The pronouns refer to particular individuals whose gender is known. The nouns are not generic.
(b) *A student* walked into the room. *He* was looking for the teacher.	
(c) *A student* should always do *his* assignments.	A GENERIC NOUN* does not refer to any person or thing in particular; rather, it represents a whole group.
	In (c): *A student* is a generic noun; it refers to *anyone who is a student.*
(d) *A student* should always do *his or her* assignments.	With a generic noun, a singular masculine pronoun has been used traditionally, but many English speakers now use both masculine and feminine pronouns to refer to a singular generic noun, as in (d).
(e) *Students* should always do *their* assignments.	Problems with choosing masculine and/or feminine pronouns can often be avoided by using a plural rather than a singular generic noun, as in (e).

Indefinite pronouns

everyone	someone	anyone	no one**
everybody	somebody	anybody	nobody
everything	something	anything	nothing

(f) *Somebody* left *his* book on the desk.	In formal English, the use of a singular pronoun to refer to an INDEFINITE PRONOUN is generally considered to be grammatically correct, as in (f) and (g).
(g) *Everyone* has *his or her* own ideas.	
(h) *INFORMAL:* *Somebody* left *their* book on the desk. *Everyone* has *their* own ideas.	In everyday, informal English (and sometimes even in more formal English), a plural personal pronoun is usually used to refer to an indefinite pronoun, as in (h).

*See Chart 7-7, p. 33, for basic article usage.

**No one* can also be written with a hyphen in British English: *No-one* heard me.

8-3 Personal Pronouns: Agreement with Collective Nouns

(a) My *family* is large. *It* is composed of nine members.	When a collective noun refers to a single impersonal unit, a singular gender-neutral pronoun (*it, its*) is used, as in (a).
(b) My *family* is loving and supportive. *They* are always ready to help me.	When a collective noun refers to a collection of various individuals, a plural pronoun (*they, them, their*) is used, as in (b).*

Examples of collective nouns

audience	couple	family	public
class	crowd	government	staff
committee	faculty	group	team

*NOTE: When the collective noun refers to a collection of individuals, the verb may be either singular or plural: *My family is* OR *are loving and supportive.* A singular verb is generally preferred in American English. A plural verb is used more frequently in British English, especially with the words *government* or *public.* (American: *The government is* planning many changes. British: *The government are* planning many changes.)

8-4 Reflexive Pronouns

Singular	**Plural**
myself	*ourselves*
yourself	*yourselves*
herself, himself, itself, oneself	*themselves*

(a) Larry was in the theater. *I saw him.* I talked *to him.*	Compare (a) and (b): Usually an object pronoun is used as the object of a verb or preposition, as ***him*** in (a). (See Chart 8-1.)
(b) *I saw myself* in the mirror. *I* looked *at myself* for a long time.	A reflexive pronoun is used as the object of a verb or preposition when the subject of the sentence and the object are the same person, as in (b).* *I* and ***myself*** are the same person.
(c) INCORRECT: I saw ~me~ in the mirror.	
— Did someone email the report to Mr. Lee? — Yes. — Are you sure? (d) — Yes. *I myself* emailed the report to him. (e) — *I* emailed the report to him *myself*.	Reflexive pronouns are also used for emphasis. In (d): The speaker would say "I myself" strongly, with emphasis. The emphatic reflexive pronoun can immediately follow a noun or pronoun, as in (d), or come at the end of the clause, as in (e).
(f) Anna lives *by herself*.	The expression ***by*** + *a reflexive pronoun* means "alone."

*Sometimes an object pronoun is used as the object of a preposition even when the subject and object pronoun are the same person. Examples: *I* took my books with **me**. **Bob** brought his books with **him**. *I looked around **me**. **She** kept her son close to **her**.*

8-5 Using *You, One,* and *They* as Impersonal Pronouns

(a) *One* should always be polite. (b) How does *one* get to Fifth Avenue from here?	In (a) and (b): ***One*** means "any person, people in general." In (c) and (d): ***You*** means "any person, people in general." ***One*** is much more formal than ***you***. Impersonal ***you***, rather than ***one***, is used more frequently in everyday English.
(c) *You* should always be polite. (d) How do *you* get to Fifth Avenue from here?	
(e) Iowa is an agricultural state. *They* grow a lot of corn there.	***They*** is used as an impersonal pronoun in spoken or very informal English to mean "people in general" or "an undefined group of people." ***They*** has no stated antecedent. Often the antecedent is implied. In (e): ***They*** = farmers in Iowa

8-6 Forms of *Other*

	Adjective	Pronoun	
Singular Plural	*another* book (is) *other* book**s** (are)	*another* (is) *other***s** (are)	Forms of ***other*** are used as either adjectives or pronouns. Notice: • ***Another*** is always singular. • A final ***-s*** is used only for a plural pronoun (***others***).
Singular Plural	*the other* book (is) *the other* book**s** (are)	*the other* (is) *the other***s** (are)	

(a) The students in the class come from many countries. One of the students is from Mexico. *Another student is* from Iraq. *Another is* from Japan. *Other students are* from Brazil. *Others are* from Algeria.	The meaning of ***another***: "one more in addition to or different from the one(s) already mentioned." The meaning of ***other***/***others*** (without ***the***): "several more in addition to or different from the one(s) already mentioned."
(b) I have three books. Two are mine. *The other book* is yours. (*The other* is yours.) (c) I have three books. One is mine. *The other books* are yours. (*The others* are yours.)	The meaning of ***the other***(s): "all that remains from a given number; the rest of a specific group."
(d) I will be here for *another three years*. (e) I need *another five dollars*. (f) We drove *another ten miles*.	***Another*** is used as an adjective with expressions of time, money, and distance, even if these expressions contain plural nouns. ***Another*** means "an additional" in these expressions.

Some of the people are waving flags. ***Others*** are not.
The motorcade has to go ***another*** mile before it reaches the embassy.

(a) Mike and I write to *each other* every week. We write to *one another* every week.	***Each other*** and ***one another*** indicate a reciprocal relationship.* In (a): I write to him every week, and he writes to me every week.
(b) Please write on *every other* line.	***Every other*** can give the idea of "alternate." The meaning in (b) means: Write on the first line. Do not write on the second line. Write on the third line. Do not write on the fourth line. (Etc.)
(c) — Have you seen Ali recently? — Yes. I saw him just *the other day*.	***The other*** is used in time expressions such as *the other day, the other morning, the other week, etc.,* to refer to the recent past. In (c): ***the other day*** means "a few days ago, not long ago."
(d) The ducklings walked in a line behind the mother duck. Then the mother duck slipped into the pond. The ducklings followed her. They slipped into the water *one after the other*. (e) They slipped into the water *one after another*.	In (d): ***one after the other*** expresses the idea that separate actions occurred very close in time. In (e): ***one after another*** has the same meaning as ***one after the other***.
(f) No one knows my secret *other than* Rosa. (g) No one knows my secret *except* (*for*) Rosa.	***Other than*** is usually used after a negative to mean "except," as in (f). Example (g) has the same meaning as (f).
(h) Fruit and vegetables are full of vitamins and minerals. *In other words,* they are good for you.	In (h): ***In other words*** is used to explain, usually in simpler or clearer terms, the meaning of the preceding sentence(s).

*In typical usage, *each other* and *one another* are interchangeable; there is no difference between them. Some native speakers, however, use *each other* when they are talking about only two persons or things, and *one another* when there are more than two.

Chapter 9
Modals, Part 1

9-1 Basic Modal Introduction

Modal auxiliaries generally express speakers' attitudes. For example, modals can express that a speaker feels something is necessary, advisable, permissible, possible, or probable; and, in addition, they can convey the strength of those attitudes. Each modal has more than one meaning or use. See Chart 10-10, p. 56−57, for a summary overview of modals.

Modal auxiliaries in English

can	had better	might	ought (to)	should	would
could	may	must	shall	will	

Modal Auxiliaries

I
You
He
She
It
We
You
They

+

can do it.
could do it.
had better do it.
may do it.
might do it.
must do it.
ought to do it.
shall do it.
should do it.
will do it.
would do it.

Modals do not take a final **-s**, even when the subject is *she, he,* or *it.*
   CORRECT: **She can** do it.
   INCORRECT: She ~~cans~~ do it.

Modals are followed immediately by the simple form of a verb.
   CORRECT: **She can do it.**
   INCORRECT: She can ~~to~~ do it. / She can ~~does~~ it. / She can ~~did~~ it.

The only exception is *ought*, which is followed by an infinitive (*to* + *the simple form of a verb*).
   CORRECT: He **ought to go** to the meeting.

Phrasal Modals

be able to do it
be going to do it
be supposed to do it
have to do it
have got to do it

Phrasal modals are common expressions whose meanings are similar to those of some of the modal auxiliaries. For example: **be able to** is similar to **can**; **be going to** is similar to **will**.

An infinitive (**to** + *the simple form of a verb*) is used in these similar expressions.

9-2 Polite Requests with *"I"* as the Subject

May I Could I	(a) *May I borrow* your pen (please)? (b) *Could I* (please) *borrow* your pen?	*May I* and *could I* are used to request permission. They are equally polite, but *may I* sounds more formal.* NOTE in (b): In a polite request, *could* has a present or future meaning, not a past meaning.
Can I	(c) *Can I borrow* your pen?	*Can I* is used informally to request permission, especially if the speaker is talking to someone she/he knows fairly well. *Can I* is usually considered a little less polite than *may I* or *could I*.
	TYPICAL RESPONSES Certainly. Yes, certainly. Of course. Yes, of course. *INFORMAL:* Sure.	Often the response to a polite request is an action, such as a nod or shake of the head, or a simple "uh-huh," meaning "yes."

*Might is also possible: *Might I borrow* your pen? *Might I* is quite formal and polite; it is used much less frequently than *may I* or *could I*.

9-3 Polite Requests with *"You"* as the Subject

Would you Will you	(a) *Would you pass* the salt (please)? (b) *Will you* (please) *pass* the salt?	The meaning of *would you* and *will you* in a polite request is the same. *Would you* is more common and is often considered more polite. The degree of politeness, however, is often determined by the speaker's tone of voice.
Could you	(c) *Could you pass* the salt (please)?	Basically, *could you* and *would you* have the same meaning. The difference is slight. *Would you* = Do you want to do this please? *Could you* = Do you want to do this please, and is it possible for you to do this? *Could you* and *would you* are equally polite.
Can you	(d) *Can you* (please) *pass* the salt?	*Can you* is often used informally. It usually sounds a little less polite than *could you* or *would you*.
	TYPICAL RESPONSES Yes, I'd (I would) be happy to / be glad to. Certainly. *INFORMAL:* Sure.	A person usually responds in the affirmative to a polite request. If a negative response is necessary, a person might begin by saying, "I'd like to, but . . ." (e.g., "I'd like to pass the salt, but I can't reach it.").
	(e) *INCORRECT:* May ~~you~~ pass the salt?	*May* is used only with *I* or *we* in polite requests.

9-4 Polite Requests with *Would You Mind*

Asking Permission

(a) *Would you mind **if I closed** the window?* (b) *Would you mind **if I used** the phone?* TYPICAL RESPONSES No, not at all. No, of course not. No, that would be fine.	Notice in (a): **Would you mind if I** is followed by the simple past.* The meaning in (a): *May I close the window? Is it all right if I close the window? Will it cause you any trouble or discomfort if I close the window?* Notice that the typical response is "no." "Yes" means *Yes, I mind.* In other words: *It is a problem for me.* Another typical response might be "unh-uh," meaning "no."

Asking Someone to Do Something

(c) *Would you mind **closing** the window?* (d) Excuse me. *Would you mind **repeating** that?* TYPICAL RESPONSES No. I'd be happy to. Not at all. I'd be glad to. *INFORMAL:* No problem. / Sure. / Okay.	Notice in (c): **Would you mind** is followed by the **-ing** form of a verb (a gerund). The meaning in (c): *I don't want to cause you any trouble, but would you please close the window? Would that cause you any inconvenience?* The informal responses "Sure" and "Okay" are common but not logical. The speaker means *No, I wouldn't mind* but seems to be saying the opposite: *Yes, I would mind.* Native speakers understand that the response "Sure" or "Okay" in this situation means that the speaker agrees to the request.

*Sometimes, in informal spoken English, the simple present is used: *Would you mind if I **close** the window?*

NOTE: The simple past does not refer to past time after **would you mind**; it refers to present or future time. See Chart 20-3, p. 105, for more information.

*Would you mind **handing** me that book?*

9-5 Expressing Necessity: *Must, Have To, Have Got To*

Must, Have To

(a) All applicants *must take* an entrance exam.	*Must* and *have to* both express necessity. The meaning is the same in (a) and (b): *It is necessary for every applicant to take an entrance exam. There is no other choice. The exam is required.*
(b) All applicants *have to take* an entrance exam.	
(c) I'm looking for Sue. I *have to talk* to her about our lunch date tomorrow. I can't meet her for lunch because I have to go to a business meeting at 1:00.	In everyday statements of necessity, *have to* is used more commonly than *must*. *Must* is usually stronger than *have to* and can indicate urgency or stress importance. The meaning in (c): *I need to do this, and I need to do that.*
(d) Where's Sue? I *must talk* to her right away. I have an urgent message for her.	The meaning in (d) is stronger: *This is very important!* Because it is a strong word, *must* (meaning necessity) is relatively rare in conversation. It is usually found in legal or academic writing.
(e) I *have to* ("hafta") be home by eight.	NOTE: Native speakers often say "hafta" and "hasta," as in (e) and (f).
(f) He *has to* ("hasta") go to a meeting tonight.	

Have Got To

(g) I *have got to go* now. I have a class in ten minutes.	*Have got to* also expresses the idea of necessity: (g) and (h) have the same meaning. *Have got to* is informal and is used primarily in spoken English. *Have to* is used in both formal and informal English.
(h) I *have to go* now. I have a class in ten minutes.	
(i) I *have got to go* ("I've gotta go / I gotta go") now.	The usual pronunciation of *got to* is "gotta." Sometimes *have* is dropped in speech: "I gotta do it."

Past Necessity

(j) PRESENT or FUTURE I *have to / have got to / must study* tonight.	*Had to* expresses past necessity. In (j): *had to* = *needed to: I needed to study last night.*
(k) PAST I *had to study* last night.	There is no other past form for *must* (when it means necessity) or *have got to*.

9-6 Lack of Necessity and Prohibition: *Have To* and *Must* in the Negative

Lack of Necessity

(a) Tomorrow is a holiday. We *don't have to go* to class.	When used in the negative, **must** and **have to** have different meanings.
(b) I can hear you. You *don't have to shout*.*	Negative form: **do not have to** = lack of necessity.
	The meaning in (a): *We don't need to go to class tomorrow because it is a holiday.*

Prohibition

(c) You *must not tell* anyone my secret. Do you promise?	**must not** = prohibition (DO NOT DO THIS!)
	The meaning in (c): *Do not tell anyone my secret. I forbid it. Telling anyone my secret is prohibited.*
	Negative contraction: **mustn't**. (The first "t" is silent: "muss-ənt.")
(d) *Don't tell* anyone my secret.	Because **must not** is so strong, speakers also express
(e) You *can't tell* anyone my secret.	prohibition with imperatives, as in (d), or with other
(f) You *'d better not tell* anyone my secret.	modals, as in (e) and (f).

*Lack of necessity may also be expressed by **need not** + *the simple form of a verb*: You **needn't shout**. The use of **needn't** as an auxiliary is chiefly British except in certain common expressions such as *You needn't worry*.

Jason   Jim

Jason **doesn't have to retake** his math exam, but Jim does.

9-7 Advisability: *Should, Ought To, Had Better*

(a) You ***should study*** harder. You ***ought to study*** harder. (b) Drivers ***should obey*** the speed limit. Drivers ***ought to obey*** the speed limit.	***Should*** and ***ought to*** both express advisability. Their meaning ranges in strength from a suggestion (*This is a good idea*) to a statement about responsibility or duty (*This is a very important thing to do*). The meaning in (a): *This is a good idea. This is my advice.* In (b): *This is an important responsibility.*
(c) You ***shouldn't leave*** your keys in the car.	Negative contraction: ***shouldn't.***★ NOTE: the /t/ is often hard to hear in relaxed, spoken English.
(d) I ***ought to*** ("otta") ***study*** tonight, but I think I'll watch TV instead.	Native speakers often pronounce ***ought to*** as "otta" in informal speech.
(e) The gas tank is almost empty. We ***had better stop*** at the next gas station. (f) You ***had better take*** care of that cut on your hand soon, or it will get infected.	In meaning, ***had better*** is close to ***should*** and ***ought to***, but ***had better*** is usually stronger. Often ***had better*** implies a warning or a threat of possible bad consequences. The meaning in (e): *If we don't stop at a service station, there will be a bad result. We will run out of gas.* Notes on the use of ***had better***: • It has a present or future meaning. • It is followed by the simple form of a verb. • It is more common in speaking than writing.
(g) You ***'d better*** take care of it. (h) You ***better*** take care of it.	Contraction: ***'d better,*** as in (g). Sometimes in speaking, ***had*** is dropped, as in (h).
(i) You ***'d better not*** be late.	Negative form: ***had better*** + ***not***

★***Ought to*** is not commonly used in the negative. If it is, the ***to*** is sometimes dropped: *You* ***oughtn't (to) leave*** *your keys in the car.*

9-8 The Past Form of *Should*

(a) I had a test this morning. I didn't do well on the test because I didn't study for it last night. I ***should have studied*** last night. (b) You were supposed to be here at 10:00 P.M., but you didn't come until midnight. We were worried about you. You ***should have called*** us. (You did not call.)	Past form: ***should have*** + *past participle.*★ The meaning in (a): ***I should have studied*** = *Studying was a good idea, but I didn't do it. I made a mistake.* Usual pronunciation of ***should have***: "should-əv" or "should-ə."
(c) My back hurts. I ***should not have carried*** that heavy box up two flights of stairs. (I carried the box, and now I'm sorry.) (d) We went to a movie, but it was a waste of time and money. We ***should not have gone*** to the movie.	The meaning in (c): ***I should not have carried*** = I carried something, but it turned out to be a bad idea. I made a mistake. Usual pronunciation of ***should not have***: "shouldn't-əv" or "shouldn't-ə."

★The past form of ***ought to*** is ***ought to have*** + *past participle* (*I ought to have studied.*). It has the same meaning as the past form of ***should***. In the past, ***should*** is used more commonly than ***ought to***. ***Had better*** is used only rarely in a past form (e.g., *He* ***had better have taken care*** *of it.*) and usually only in speaking, not writing.

9-9 Obligation: *Be Supposed To*

(a) The game *is supposed to begin* at 10:00. (b) The committee *is supposed to vote* by secret ballot.	**Be supposed to** expresses the idea that someone (*I, we, they, the teacher, lots of people, my father, etc.*) expects something to happen. **Be supposed to** often expresses expectations about scheduled events, as in (a), or correct procedures, as in (b).
(c) I *am supposed to go* to the meeting. My boss told me that he wants me to attend. (d) The children *are supposed to put away* their toys before they go to bed.	**Be supposed to** also expresses expectations about behavior. The meaning is the same in (c) and (d): *Someone else expects (requests or requires) certain behavior.*
(e) Jack *was supposed to call* me last night. I wonder why he didn't.	**Be supposed to** in the past (*was/were supposed to*) expresses unfulfilled expectations. The meaning in (e): *I expected Jack to call, but he didn't.*

9-10 Unfulfilled Intentions: *Was/Were Going To*

(a) I'*m going to go* to the concert tomorrow. I'm really looking forward to it.	**Am/is/are going to** is used to talk about intentions for future activities, as in (a).
(b) Jack *was going to go* to the movie last night, but he changed his mind.	**Was/were going to** talks about past intentions. Usually, these are unfulfilled intentions, i.e., activities someone intended to do but did not do. The meaning in (b): *Jack was planning to go to the concert, but he didn't go.*
(c) I *was planning* to go, but I didn't. I *was hoping* to go, but I couldn't. I *was intending* to go, but I didn't. I *was thinking about* going, but I didn't. (d) I *had hoped* to go, but I couldn't. I *had intended* to go, but I didn't. I *had thought about* going, but I didn't. I *had planned* to go, but I changed my mind.	Other ways of expressing unfulfilled intentions are to use **plan**, **hope**, **intend**, and **think about** in the past progressive, as in (c), or in the past perfect, as in (d).

9-11 Making Suggestions: *Let's, Why Don't, Shall I / We*

(a) **Let's go** to a movie.	**let's** = **let us** **Let's** is followed by the simple form of a verb.
(b) **Let's not go** to a movie. **Let's stay** home instead.	Negative form: **let's** + **not** + *simple verb* **Let's** means *I have a suggestion for us.*
(c) **Why don't we go** to a movie? (d) **Why don't you come** around seven? (e) **Why don't I give** Mary a call?	**Why don't** is used primarily in spoken English to make a friendly suggestion. The meaning in (c): *Let's go to a movie.* In (d): *I suggest that you come around seven.* In (e): *Should I give Mary a call? Do you agree with my suggestion?*
(f) **Shall I open** the window? Is that okay with you? (g) **Shall we leave** at two? Is that okay?	When **shall** is used with **I** or **we** in a question, the speaker is usually making a suggestion and asking another person if she/he agrees with this suggestion, as in (f) and (g). The use of **shall** + **I/we** is relatively formal and infrequent in American English.
(h) Let's go, **shall we?** (i) Let's go, **okay?**	Sometimes **shall we?** is used as a tag question after **let's**, as in (h). More informally, **okay?** is used as a tag question, as in (i).

Why don't we go to the soccer game tomorrow?
Let's not sit here all afternoon.
Let's go to a museum this afternoon, **shall we?**

9-12 Making Suggestions: *Could* vs. *Should*

— *What should we do tomorrow?* (a) Why don't we go on a picnic? (b) We *could go* on a picnic.	**Could** can be used to make suggestions. The meanings in (a) and (b) are similar: The speaker is suggesting a picnic.
— *I'm having trouble in math class.* (c) You *should talk* to your teacher. (d) *Maybe* you *should talk* to your teacher. — *I'm having trouble in math class.* (e) You *could talk* to your teacher. Or you *could ask* Ann to help you with your math lessons. Or I *could try* to help you.	**Should** gives definite advice and is stronger than **could**. The meaning in (c): *I believe it is important for you to do this. This is what I recommend.* In (d), the use of **maybe** softens the strength of the advice. **Could** offers suggestions or possibilities. The meaning in (e): *I have some possible suggestions for you. It is possible to do this. Or it is possible to do that.**
— *I failed my math class.* (f) You *should have talked* to your teacher and gotten some help from her during the term. — *I failed my math class.* (g) You *could have talked* to your teacher. Or you *could have asked* Ann to help you with your math. Or I *could have tried* to help you.	**Should have** (past form) gives "hindsight" advice.**** The meaning in (f): *It was important for you to talk to the teacher, but you didn't do it. You made a mistake.* **Could have** (past form) offers "hindsight" possibilities. The meaning in (g): *You had the chance to do this or that. It was possible for this or that to happen. You missed some good opportunities.*

***Might** (but not **may**) can also be used to make suggestions (*You **might** talk to your teacher.*), but **could** is more common.

**Hindsight refers to looking back at something after it happens.

Carl   Alice   Roberto

Chapter 10

Modals, Part 2

10-1	Degrees of Certainty: Present Time

— Why isn't John in class? **100% sure**: He *is* sick. **95% sure**: He *must be* sick. **50% sure or less**: { He *may be* sick. He *might be* sick. He *could be* sick. NOTE: These percentages are approximate.	*Degree of certainty* refers to how sure we are — what we think the chances are — that something is true. If we are sure something is true in the present, we don't need to use a modal. For example, if I say, "John is sick," I am sure; I am stating a fact that I am sure is true. My degree of certainty is 100%.
— Why isn't John in class? (a) He *must be* sick. (Usually he is in class every day, but when I saw him last night, he wasn't feeling good. So my best guess is that he is sick today. I can't think of another possibility.)	*Must* expresses a strong degree of certainty about a present situation, but the degree of certainty is still less than 100%. In (a): The speaker is saying, "Probably John is sick. I have evidence to make me believe that he is sick. That is my logical conclusion, but I do not know for certain."
— Why isn't John in class? (b) He *may be* sick. (c) He *might be* sick. (d) He *could be* sick. (I don't really know. He may be at home watching TV. He might be at the library. He could be out of town.)	*May*, *might*, and *could* express a weak degree of certainty. In (b), (c), and (d): The meanings are all the same. The speaker is saying, "Perhaps, maybe,* possibly John is sick. I am only making a guess. I can think of other possibilities."

***Maybe** (one word) is an adverb: **Maybe** *he is sick*. **May be** (two words) is a verb form: *He* **may be** *sick*.

10-2 Degrees of Certainty: Present Time Negative

100% sure:	Sam *isn't* hungry.
99% sure:	Sam *couldn't be* hungry. Sam *can't be* hungry.
95% sure:	Sam *must not be* hungry.
50% sure or less:	Sam *may not be* hungry. Sam *might not be* hungry.

NOTE: These percentages are approximate.

(a) Sam doesn't want anything to eat. He *isn't* hungry. He told me his stomach is full. I heard him say that he isn't hungry. I believe him.	In (a): The speaker is sure that Sam is not hungry.
(b) Sam *couldn't/can't be* hungry. That's impossible. I just saw him eat a huge meal. He has already eaten enough to fill two grown men! Did he really say he'd like something to eat? I don't believe it.	In (b): The speaker believes that there is no possibility that Sam is hungry (but the speaker is not 100% sure). When used in the negative to show degree of certainty, *couldn't* and *can't* forcefully express the idea that the speaker believes something is impossible.
(c) Sam isn't eating his food. He *must not be* hungry. That's the only reason I can think of.	In (c): The speaker is expressing a logical conclusion, a "best guess."
(d) I don't know why Sam isn't eating his food. He *may not/might not be* hungry right now. Or maybe he doesn't feel well. Or perhaps he ate just before he got here. Who knows?	In (d): The speaker uses *may not/might not* to mention a possibility.

10-3 Degrees of Certainty: Past Time

Past Time: Affirmative

	— *Why wasn't Mary in class?*		In (a): The speaker is sure.
(a)	**100%:**	She *was* sick.	In (b): The speaker is making a logical conclusion, e.g., "I saw Mary yesterday and found out that she was sick. I assume that is the reason why she was absent. I can't think of any other good reason."
(b)	**95%:**	She *must have been* sick.	
(c)	**50% sure or less:**	She *may have been* sick. She *might have been* sick. She *could have been* sick.	In (c): The speaker is mentioning one possibility.

Past Time: Negative

	— *Why didn't Sam eat?*		In (d): The speaker is sure.
(d)	**100%:**	Sam *wasn't* hungry.	In (e): The speaker believes that it is impossible for Sam to have been hungry.
(e)	**99%:**	Sam *couldn't have been* hungry. Sam *can't have been* hungry.	
(f)	**95%:**	Sam *must not have been* hungry.	In (f): The speaker is making a logical conclusion.
(g)	**50% sure or less:**	Sam *may not have been* hungry. Sam *might not have been* hungry.	In (g): The speaker is mentioning one possibility.

10-4 Degrees of Certainty: Future Time

100% sure:	Kay *will do* well on the test.	→	The speaker feels sure.
90% sure:	Kay *should do* well on the test. Kay *ought to do* well on the test.	→	The speaker is almost sure.
50% sure or less:	She *may do* well on the test. She *might do* well on the test. She *could do* well on the test.	→	The speaker is guessing.

(a) Kay has been studying hard. She *should do/ought to do* well on the test tomorrow.	***Should/ought to*** can be used to express expectations about future events. In (a): The speaker is saying, "Kay will probably do well on the test. I expect her to do well. That is what I think will happen."
(b) I wonder why Sue hasn't written us. We *should have heard / ought to have heard* from her last week.	The past form of ***should/ought to*** is used to mean that the speaker expected something that did not occur.

10-5 Progressive Forms of Modals

(a) Let's just knock on the door lightly. Tom *may be sleeping*. (*right now*)	Progressive form, present time: modal + ***be*** + ***-ing*** Meaning: *in progress right now*
(b) All of the lights in Ann's room are turned off. She *must be sleeping*. (*right now*)	
(c) Sue wasn't at home last night when we went to visit her. She *might have been studying* at the library.	Progressive form, past time: modal + ***have been*** + ***-ing*** Meaning: *in progress at a time in the past*
(d) Joe wasn't at home last night. He has a lot of exams coming up soon, and he is also working on a term paper. He *must have been studying* at the library.	

The students *may be having* fun,
but they *shouldn't be climbing* out the windows!

10-6 Ability: *Can* and *Could*

(a) Tom is strong. He *can lift* that heavy box.	*Can* is used to express physical ability, as in (a).
(b) I *can see* Central Park from my apartment.	*Can* is frequently used with verbs of the five senses: *see, hear, feel, smell, taste*, as in (b).
(c) Maria *can play* the piano. She's been taking lessons for many years.	*Can* is used to express an acquired skill. In (c): *can play = knows how to play.*
(d) You *can buy* a hammer at the hardware store.	*Can* is used to express possibility. In (d): *you can buy = it is possible for one to buy.*
COMPARE: (e) I'm not quite ready to go, but you *can leave* if you're in a hurry. I'll meet you later. (f) When you finish the test, you *may leave*.	*Can* is used to give permission in informal situations, as in (e). In formal situations, *may* rather than *can* is usually used to give permission, as in (f).
(g) Dogs *can bark*, but they *cannot/can't talk*.	Negative form: *cannot* or *can't*
(h) Tom *could lift* the box, but I *couldn't*.	The past form of *can* meaning "ability" is *could*, as in (h). Negative form: *could not* or *couldn't*

10-7 Using *Would* to Express a Repeated Action in the Past

(a) When I was a child, my father *would read* me a story at night before bedtime. (b) When I was a child, my father *used to read* me a story at night before bedtime.	*Would* can be used to express *an action that was repeated regularly in the past*. When *would* is used to express this idea, it has the same meaning as *used to* (*habitual past*). Sentences (a) and (b) have the same meaning.
(c) I *used to live* in California. He *used to be* a Boy Scout. They *used to have* a Ford.	*Used to* expresses *a situation that existed in the past*, as in (c). In this case, *would* may not be used as an alternative. *Would* is used only for regularly repeated *actions* in the past.

10-8 Expressing Preference: *Would Rather*

(a) I *would rather go* to a movie tonight *than study* grammar. (b) I*'d rather study* history *than* (*study*) biology.	*Would rather* expresses preference. In (a): Notice that the simple form of a verb follows both *would rather* and *than*. In (b): If the verb is the same, it usually is not repeated after *than*.
— *How much do you weigh?* (c) I*'d rather not tell* you.	Contraction: *I would* = *I'd* Negative form: *would rather* + *not*
(d) The movie was okay, but I *would rather have gone* to the concert last night.	The past form: *would rather have* + *past participle*. Usual pronunciation: "I'd rather-əv"
(e) I*'d rather be lying* on a beach in India than (*be*) *sitting* in class right now.	Progressive form: *would rather* + *be* + *-ing*

10-9 Combining Modals with Phrasal Modals

(a) *INCORRECT:* Janet will ~~can~~ help you tomorrow.	A modal cannot be immediately followed by another modal. In (a): The modal *will* cannot be followed by *can*, which is another modal.
(b) Janet *will be able to* help you tomorrow. (c) You *will have to* pick her up at her home.	A modal can, however, be followed by the phrasal modals *be able to* and *have to*. In (b): The modal *will* is correctly followed by the phrasal modal *be able to*.
(d) Tom *isn't going to be able to* help you tomorrow.	It is also sometimes possible for one phrasal modal to follow another phrasal modal. In (d): *be going to* is followed by *be able to*. This form is more common in negatives and questions.

10-10 Summary Chart of Modals and Similar Expressions

Auxiliary	Uses	Present/Future	Past
may	(1) polite request (only with "I" or "we")	*May* I *borrow* your pen?	
	(2) formal permission	You *may leave* the room.	
	(3) 50% or less certainty	— *Where's John?* He *may be* at the library.	He *may have been* at the library.
might	(1) 50% or less certainty	— *Where's John?* He *might be* at the library.	He *might have been* at the library.
	(2) polite request (*rare*)	*Might* I *borrow* your pen?	
should	(1) advisability	I *should study* tonight.	I *should have studied* last night, but I didn't.
	(2) 90% certainty (*expectation*)	She *should do* well on the test tomorrow.	She *should have done* well on the test.
ought to	(1) advisability	I *ought to study* tonight.	I *ought to have studied* last night, but I didn't.
	(2) 90% certainty (*expectation*)	She *ought to do* well on the test tomorrow.	She *ought to have done* well on the test.
had better	(1) advisability with threat of bad result	You *had better be* on time, or we will leave without you.	(*past form uncommon*)
be supposed to	(1) expectation	Class *is supposed to begin* at 10:00.	
	(2) unfulfilled expectation		Class *was supposed to begin* at 10:00, but it began at 10:15.
must	(1) strong necessity	I *must go* to class today.	(I *had to go* to class yesterday.)
	(2) prohibition (*negative*)	You *must not* open that door.	
	(3) 95% certainty	Mary isn't in class. She *must be* sick.	Mary *must have been* sick yesterday.
have to	(1) necessity	I *have to go* to class today.	I *had to go* to class yesterday.
	(2) lack of necessity (*negative*)	I *don't have to go* to class today.	I *didn't have to go* to class yesterday.
have got to	(1) necessity	I *have got to go* to class today.	(I *had to go* to class yesterday.)
will	(1) 100% certainty	He *will be* here at 6:00.	
	(2) willingness	— *The phone's ringing.* I*'ll get* it.	
	(3) polite request	*Will* you please help me?	
be going to	(1) 100% certainty (*prediction*)	He *is going to be* here at 6:00.	
	(2) definite plan (*intention*)	I*'m going to paint* my bedroom.	
	(3) unfulfilled intention		I *was going to paint* my room, but I didn't have time.

Auxiliary	Uses	Present/Future	Past
can	(1) ability/possibility	I *can run* fast.	I *could run* fast when I was a child, but now I can't.
	(2) informal permission	You *can use* my car tomorrow.	
	(3) informal polite request	*Can* I *borrow* your pen?	
	(4) impossibility (*negative only*)	That *can't be* true!	That *can't have been* true!
could	(1) past ability		I *could run* fast when I was a child.
	(2) polite request	*Could* I *borrow* your pen? *Could* you *help* me?	
	(3) suggestion (*affirmative only*)	— I *need help in math*. You *could talk* to your teacher.	You *could have talked* to your teacher.
	(4) 50% or less certainty	— *Where's John?* He *could be* at home.	He *could have been* at home.
	(5) impossibility (*negative only*)	That *couldn't be* true!	That *couldn't have been* true!
be able to	(1) ability	I *am able to help* you. I *will be able to help* you.	I *was able to help* him.
would	(1) polite request	*Would* you please *help* me? *Would* you *mind* if I left early?	
	(2) preference	I *would rather go* to the park than *stay* home.	I *would rather have gone* to the park.
	(3) repeated action in the past		When I was a child, I *would visit* my grandparents every weekend.
	(4) polite for "want" (with "like")	I *would like* an apple, please.	
	(5) unfulfilled wish		I *would have liked* a cookie, but there were none in the house.
used to	(1) repeated action in the past.		I *used to visit* my grandparents every weekend.
	(2) past situation that no longer exists		I *used to live* in Spain. Now I live in Korea.
shall	(1) polite question to make a suggestion	*Shall* I *open* the window?	
	(2) future with *I* or *we* as subject	I *shall arrive* at nine. ("will" = more common)	

NOTE: The use of modals in reported speech is discussed in Chart 12-7, p. 67. The use of modals in conditional sentences is discussed in Chapter 20.

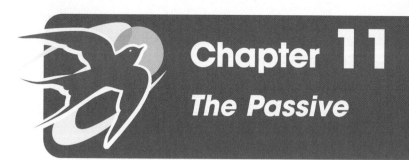

Chapter 11
The Passive

11-1 Active vs. Passive

 Active: (a) subject: Mary verb: *helped* object: the boy. Passive: (b) subject: The boy verb: *was helped* by Mary.	In the passive, *the object* of an active verb becomes *the subject* of the passive verb: **the boy** in (a) becomes the subject of the passive verb in (b). Notice that the subject of an active verb follows **by** in a passive sentence. The noun that follows **by** is called the "agent." In (b): **Mary** is the agent. Sentences (a) and (b) have the same meaning.

Passive: **be**   +   *past participle*
     (c)   He   *is*   *helped*   by her.
           He   *was*   *helped*   by her.
           He   *will be*   *helped*   by her.
	Form of the passive: **be** + *past participle*

Active: (d) An accident *happened.* Passive: (e) (none)	Only transitive verbs (verbs that can be followed by an object) are used in the passive. It is not possible to use intransitive verbs (such as *happen, sleep, come, seem, die*) in the passive. (See Appendix Chart A-1.)

11-2 Tense Forms of the Passive

	Active			Passive			
(a) simple present	Mary	*helps*	the boy.	The boy	*is*	*helped*	by Mary.
(b) present progressive	Mary	*is helping*	the boy.	The boy	*is being*	*helped*	by Mary.
(c) present perfect*	Mary	*has helped*	the boy.	The boy	*has been*	*helped*	by Mary.
(d) simple past	Mary	*helped*	the boy.	The boy	*was*	*helped*	by Mary.
(e) past progressive	Mary	*was helping*	the boy.	The boy	*was being*	*helped*	by Mary.
(f) past perfect*	Mary	*had helped*	the boy.	The boy	*had been*	*helped*	by Mary.
(g) simple future	Mary	*will help*	the boy.	The boy	*will be*	*helped*	by Mary.
(h) *be going to*	Mary	*is going to help*	the boy.	The boy	*is going to be*	*helped*	by Mary.
(i) future perfect*	Mary	*will have helped*	the boy.	The boy	*will have been*	*helped*	by Mary.

(j) **Was** the boy *helped* by Mary? (k) **Has** the boy *been helped* by Mary?	In the question form of passive verbs, an auxiliary verb precedes the subject.

*The progressive forms of the *present perfect*, *past perfect*, and *future perfect* are rarely used in the passive.

11-3 Using the Passive

(a) Rice *is grown* in India. (b) Our house *was built* in 1980. (c) This olive oil *was imported* from Crete.	Usually the passive is used without a *by*-phrase. The passive is most frequently used when it is not known or not important to know exactly who performs an action. In (a): Rice is grown in India by people, by farmers, by someone. It is not known or important to know exactly who grows rice in India. Examples (a), (b), and (c) illustrate the most common use of the passive, i.e., without the *by*-phrase.
(d) My aunt *made* this rug. (*active*)	If the speaker knows who performs an action, usually the active is used, as in (d).
(e) This rug *was made* by my aunt. That rug *was made* by my mother. (f) *Life on the Mississippi was written* by Mark Twain.	Sometimes, even when the speaker knows who performs an action, he/she chooses to use the passive with the *by*-phrase in order to focus attention on the subject of a sentence. In (e): The focus of attention is on two rugs. In (f): The focus is on the book, but the *by*-phrase is included because it contains important information.

11-4 The Passive Form of Modals and Phrasal Modals

Passive form:	**modal***	+	*be*	+	**past participle**	
(a) Tom	will		be		invited	to the picnic.
(b) The window	can't		be		opened.	
(c) Children	should		be		taught	to respect their elders.
(d)	May I		be		excused	from class?
(e) This book	had better		be		returned	to the library before Friday.
(f) This letter	ought to		be		sent	before June 1st.
(g) Mary	has to		be		told	about our change in plans.
(h) Fred	is supposed to		be		told	about the meeting.

Past-passive form:	**modal**	+	*have been*	+	**past participle**	
(i) The letter	should		have been		sent	last week.
(j) This house	must		have been		built	over 200 years ago.
(k) Eric	couldn't		have been		offered	the job.
(l) Jill	ought to		have been		invited	to the party.

*See Chapters 9 and 10 for a discussion of the form and use of modals and phrasal modals.

11-5 Non-Progressive Passive

(a) The door is *old*. (b) The door is *green*. (c) The door is *locked*.	In (a) and (b): *old* and *green* are adjectives. They describe the door. In (c): *locked* is a past participle. It is used as an adjective. It describes the door.
(d) I locked the door five minutes ago. (e) The door was locked by me five minutes ago. (f) Now the door *is locked*.	When the passive form is used to describe an existing situation or state, as in (c), (f), and (i), it is called the "non-progressive passive." In the non-progressive: • no action is taking place; the action happened earlier.
(g) Ann broke the window yesterday. (h) The window was broken by Ann. (i) Now the window *is broken*.	• there is no *by*-phrase. • the past participle functions as an adjective.
(j) I *am interested in* Chinese art. (k) He *is satisfied with* his job. (l) Ann *is married to* Alex.	Prepositions other than *by* can follow non-progressive passive verbs. (See Chart 11-6.)
(m) I don't know where I am. I *am lost*. (n) I can't find my purse. It *is gone*. (o) I *am finished with* my work. (p) I *am done with* my work.	Sentences (m) through (p) are examples of idiomatic usage of the passive form in common, everyday English. These sentences have no equivalent active sentences.

11-6 Common Non-Progressive Passive Verbs + Prepositions

(a) I'm *interested in* Greek culture. (b) He's *worried about* losing his job.	Many non-progressive verbs are followed by prepositions other than *by*.

be concerned be excited be worried	} *about*	be composed be made be tired	} *of*	be acquainted be associated be cluttered	
be discriminated	*against*	be frightened be scared be terrified	} *of/by*	be crowded be done be equipped be filled	} *with*
be known be prepared be qualified be remembered be well known	} *for*	be accustomed be addicted be committed be connected be dedicated		be finished be pleased be provided be satisfied	
be divorced be exhausted be gone be protected	} *from*	be devoted be engaged be exposed be limited	} *to*	be annoyed be bored be covered	} *with/by*
be dressed be interested be located	} *in*	be married be opposed be related			
be disappointed be involved	} *in/with*				

11-7 The Passive with *Get*

Get + Adjective

(a) I'm *getting hungry*. Let's eat soon. (b) I stopped working because I *got sleepy*.	***Get*** may be followed by certain adjectives. ***Get*** gives the idea of change — the idea of becoming, beginning to be, growing to be. In (a): ***I'm getting hungry*** = I wasn't hungry before, but now I'm beginning to be hungry.

Common adjectives that follow *get*

angry	cold	fat	hungry	quiet	tall
anxious	comfortable	full	late	ready	thirsty
bald	dark	good	light	rich	warm
better	dizzy	hard	mad	ripe	well
big	easy	healthy	nervous	serious	wet
busy	empty	heavy	noisy	sick	worse
chilly	famous	hot	old	sleepy	

Get + Past Participle

(c) I stopped working because I *got tired*. (d) They *are getting married* next month.	***Get*** may also be followed by a past participle. The past participle functions as an adjective; it describes the subject. The passive with ***get*** is common in spoken English, but not in formal writing.

Common past participles with *get*

get accepted (for, into)	get dressed (in)	get invited (to)
get accustomed to	get drunk (on)	get involved (in, with)
get acquainted (with)	get elected (to)	get killed (by, with)
get arrested (for)	get engaged (to)	get lost (in)
get bored (with)	get excited (about)	get married (to)
get confused (about)	get finished (with)	get prepared (for)
get crowded (with)	get fixed (by)	get scared (of)
get divorced (from)	get hurt (by)	get sunburned
get done (with)	get interested (in)	get worried (about)

11-8 Participial Adjectives

— The problem confuses the students. (a) It is *a confusing problem*.	The *present participle* serves as an adjective with an active meaning. The noun it modifies performs an action. In (a): The noun ***problem*** does something; it *confuses*. Thus, it is described as a "confusing problem."
— The students are confused by the problem. (b) They are *confused students*.	The *past participle* serves as an adjective with a passive meaning. In (b): The students are confused by something. Thus, they are described as "confused students."
— The story amuses the children. (c) It is *an amusing story*.	In (c): The noun ***story*** performs the action.
— The children are amused by the story. (d) They are *amused children*.	In (d): The noun ***children*** receives the action.

Chapter 12
Noun Clauses

12-1 Introduction

independent clause (a) ⌐Sue lives in Tokyo.⌐	A clause is a group of words containing a subject and a verb.* An INDEPENDENT CLAUSE (or *main clause*) is a complete sentence. It contains the main subject and verb of a sentence. Examples (a) and (b) are complete sentences. Example (a) is a statement; (b) is a question.
independent clause (b) ⌐Where does Sue live?⌐	
dependent clause (c) ⌐where Sue lives⌐	A DEPENDENT CLAUSE (or *subordinate clause*) is not a complete sentence. Example (c) is a dependent clause.
noun clause (d) I know ⌐*where Sue lives.*⌐	Example (d) is a complete sentence, with a main subject (*I*) and verb (*know*) followed by a dependent clause. ***Where Sue lives*** is called a *noun clause*.
S **V** **O** (e) I **know** ⌐*what he said.*⌐ **S** **V** (f) ⌐*What he said*⌐ **is** true.	A NOUN CLAUSE has the same uses in a sentence as a noun: it is used as an object or a subject. In (e): The noun clause is the object of the verb ***know***. In (f): The noun clause is the subject of the verb ***is***.

*A *phrase* is a group of words that does NOT contain a subject and a verb.

12-2 Noun Clauses Beginning with a Question Word

Question	Noun Clause	
Where does she live? What did he say? When do they arrive?	(a) I don't know *where she lives*. (b) I couldn't hear *what he said*. (c) Do you know *when they arrive*?	In (a): *where she lives* is the object of the verb *know*. In a noun clause, the subject precedes the verb. Do not use question word order in a noun clause. Notice: *does*, *did*, and *do* are used in questions but not in noun clauses. See Appendix Chart B-2 for more information about question words and question forms.
S V Who lives there? Who is at the door?	S V (d) I don't know *who lives there*. (e) I wonder *who is at the door*.	In (d) and (e): The word order is the same in both the question and the noun clause because *who* is the subject in both.
V S Who are those men? Whose house is that?	S V (f) I don't know *who those men are*. (g) I wonder *whose house that is*.	In (f): *those men* is the subject of the question, so it is placed in front of the verb *be* in the noun clause.*
What did she say? What should they do?	(h) *What she said* surprised me. S V (i) *What they should do* is obvious.	In (h): *What she said* is the subject of the sentence. Notice in (i): A noun clause subject takes a singular verb (e.g., *is*).

*COMPARE: *Who **is** at the door?* = *who* is the subject of the question.
         *Who **are** those men?* = *those men* is the subject of the question, so *be* is plural.

12-3 Noun Clauses Beginning with *Whether* or *If*

Yes/No Question	Noun Clause	

Will she come?
 	
Does he need help?
	(a) I don't know *whether she will come*.
	     I don't know *if she will come*.
	(b) I wonder *whether he needs help*.
	     I wonder *if he needs help*.
		When a yes/no question is changed to a noun clause, *whether* or *if* is used to introduce the clause.
		
		NOTE: *Whether* is more common than *if* in formal English. Both *whether* and *if* are commonly used in speaking.

	(c) I wonder *whether or not* she will come. (d) I wonder *whether* she will come *or not*. (e) I wonder *if* she will come *or not*.	In (c), (d), and (e): Notice the patterns when *or not* is used.
	(f) *Whether she comes or not* is unimportant to me.	In (f): Notice that the noun clause is in the subject position.

12-4 Question Words Followed by Infinitives

(a) I don't know *what I should do*.
(b) I don't know **what to do**.

(c) Pam can't decide *whether she should go or stay home*.
(d) Pam can't decide **whether to go or (to) stay home**.

(e) Please tell me *how I can get to the bus station*.
(f) Please tell me **how to get to the bus station**.

(g) Jim told us *where we could find it*.
(h) Jim told us **where to find it**.

Question words (**when**, **where**, **how**, **who**, **whom**, **whose**, **what**, **which**, and **whether**) may be followed by an infinitive.

Each pair of sentences in the examples has the same meaning.

Notice that the meaning expressed by the infinitive is either **should** or **can**/**could**.

Do you know **how to get to Union Street**?
I don't know **which exit to take**.

12-5 Noun Clauses Beginning with *That*

Verb + *That*-Clause

(a) I **think** *that Bob will come.* (b) I **think** *Bob will come.*	In (a): *that Bob will come* is a noun clause. It is used as the object of the verb **think**. The word *that* is usually omitted in speaking, as in (b). It is usually included in formal writing. See the list below for verbs commonly followed by a *that*-clause.

agree that	*feel* that	*know* that	*remember* that
believe that	*find out* that	*learn* that	*say* that
decide that	*forget* that	*notice* that	*tell* someone that
discover that	*hear* that	*promise* that	*think* that
explain that	*hope* that	*read* that	*understand* that

Person + *Be* + Adjective + *That*-Clause

(c) **Jan is happy** (*that*) **Bob called.**	*That*-clauses commonly follow certain adjectives, such as *happy* in (c), when the subject refers to a person (or persons). See the list below.

I'm *afraid* that*	Al is *certain* that	We're *happy* that	Jan is *sorry* that
I'm *amazed* that	Al is *confident* that	We're *pleased* that	Jan is *sure* that
I'm *angry* that	Al is *disappointed* that	We're *proud* that	Jan is *surprised* that
I'm *aware* that	Al is *glad* that	We're *relieved* that	Jan is *worried* that

It + *Be* + Adjective + *That*-Clause

(d) **It is clear** (*that*) **Ann likes her new job.**	*That*-clauses commonly follow adjectives in sentences that begin with *it* + *be*, as in (d). See the list below.

It's *amazing* that	It's *interesting* that	It's *obvious* that	It's *true* that
It's *clear* that	It's *likely* that	It's *possible* that	It's *undeniable* that
It's *good* that	It's *lucky* that	It's *strange* that	It's *well/known* that
It's *important* that	It's *nice* that	It's *surprising* that	It's *wonderful* that

That-Clause Used as a Subject

(e) *That Ann likes her new job* **is clear.**	It is possible but uncommon for *that*-clauses to be used as the subject of a sentence, as in (e). The word *that* is not omitted when the *that*-clause is used as a subject.
(f) **The fact** (*that*) **Ann likes her new job is clear.** (g) **It is a fact** (*that*) **Ann likes her new job.**	More often, a *that*-clause in the subject position begins with **the fact that**, as in (f), or is introduced by *it is a fact*, as in (g).

To be afraid has two possible meanings:
  (1) It can express fear: *I'm afraid of dogs. I'm afraid that his dog will bite me.*
  (2) It often expresses a meaning similar to "to be sorry": *I'm afraid that I can't accept your invitation. I'm afraid you have the wrong number.*

12-6 Quoted Speech

Quoted speech refers to reproducing words exactly as they were originally spoken.* Quotation marks ("...") are used.**

Quoting One Sentence

(a) She said, "*My* brother is a student."	In (a): Use a comma after **she said**. Capitalize the first word of the quoted sentence. Put the final quotation marks outside the period at the end of the sentence.
(b) "My brother is a student," she said.	In (b): Use a comma, not a period, at the end of the quoted sentence when it precedes **she said**.
(c) "My brother," she said, "*is* a student."	In (c): If the quoted sentence is divided by **she said**, use a comma after the first part of the quote. Do not capitalize the first word after **she said**.

Quoting More Than One Sentence

(d) "My brother is a student. He is attending a university," she said.	In (d): Quotation marks are placed at the beginning and end of the complete quote. Notice: There are no quotation marks after **student**.
(e) "My brother is a student," she said. "*He* is attending a university."	In (e): Since **she said** comes between two quoted sentences, the second sentence begins with quotation marks and a capital letter.

Quoting a Question or an Exclamation

(f) She asked, "When will you be here?"	In (f): The question mark is inside the closing quotation marks.
(g) "When will you be here?" she asked.	In (g): Since a question mark is used, no comma is used before *she asked*.
(h) She said, "Watch out!"	In (h): The exclamation point is inside the closing quotation marks.
(i) "My brother is a student," *said Anna*. "My brother," *said Anna,* "is a student."	In (i): The noun subject (**Anna**) follows **said**. A noun subject often follows the verb when the subject and verb come in the middle or at the end of a quoted sentence. NOTE: A pronoun subject almost always precedes the verb. *"My brother is a student,"* **she said**. VERY RARE: *"My brother is a student,"* **said she**.
(j) "Let's leave," *whispered* Dave. (k) "Please help me," *begged* the unfortunate man. (l) "Well," Jack *began,* "it's a long story."	*Say* and *ask* are the most commonly used quote verbs. Some others: *add, agree, announce, answer, beg, begin, comment, complain, confess, continue, explain, inquire, promise, remark, reply, respond, shout, suggest, whisper.*

Quoted speech is also called "direct speech." *Reported speech* (discussed in Chart 12-7) is also called "indirect speech."

**In British English, quotation marks are called "inverted commas" and can consist of either double marks (") or a single mark ('): *She said, 'My brother is a student'.*

12-7 Reported Speech: Verb Forms in Noun Clauses

Quoted Speech	Reported Speech	
(a) "I *watch* TV every day."	→ She said she *watched* TV every day.	*Reported speech* refers to using a noun clause to report what someone has said. No quotation marks are used.
(b) "I *am watching* TV."	→ She said she *was watching* TV.	
(c) "I *have watched* TV."	→ She said she *had watched* TV.	
(d) "I *watched* TV."	→ She said she *had watched* TV.	If the reporting verb (the main verb of the sentence, e.g., *said*) is simple past, the verb in the noun clause will usually also be in a past form, as in these examples.
(e) "I *had watched* TV."	→ She said she *had watched* TV.	
(f) "I *will watch* TV."	→ She said she *would watch* TV.	
(g) "I *am going to watch* TV."	→ She said she *was going to watch* TV.	
(h) "I *can watch* TV."	→ She said she *could watch* TV.	
(i) "I *may watch* TV."	→ She said she *might watch* TV.	
(j) "I *must watch* TV."	→ She said she *had to watch* TV.	
(k) "I *have to watch* TV."	→ She said she *had to watch* TV.	
(l) "I *should watch* TV."	→ She said she *should watch* TV.	In (l): *should*, *ought to*, and *might* do not change.
"I *ought to watch* TV."	→ She said she *ought to watch* TV.	
"I *might watch* TV."	→ She said she *might watch* TV.	
(m) Immediate reporting: — What did the teacher just say? I didn't hear him. — He said he *wants* us to read Chapter 6.		Changing verbs to past forms in reported speech is common in both speaking and writing.
(n) Later reporting: — I didn't go to class yesterday. Did Mr. Jones give any assignments? — Yes. He said he *wanted* us to read Chapter 6.		However, sometimes in spoken English, no change is made in the noun clause verb, especially if the speaker is reporting something immediately or soon after it was said.
(o) "The world *is* round."	→ She said the world *is* round.	Also, sometimes the present tense is retained even in formal English when the reported sentence deals with a general truth, as in (o).
(p) "I *watch* TV every day."	→ She *says* she *watches* TV every day.	When the reporting verb is simple present, present perfect or future, the noun clause verb is not changed.
(q) "I *watch* TV every day."	→ She *has said* that she *watches* TV every day.	
(r) "I *watch* TV every day."	→ She *will say* that she *watches* TV every day.	
(s) "*Watch* TV."	→ She *told* me *to watch* TV.*	In reported speech, an imperative sentence is changed to an infinitive. *Tell* is used instead of *say* as the reporting verb. See Chart 14-6, p. 79, for other verbs followed by an infinitive that are used to report speech.

*NOTE: **Tell** is immediately followed by a (pro)noun object, but **say** is not: *He told **me** he would be late. He said he would be late.*
Also possible: *He said **to me** he would be late.*

12-8 Using -*ever* Words

The following **-*ever*** words give the idea of "any." Each pair of sentences in the examples has the same meaning.

whoever	(a) ***Whoever*** wants to come is welcome. *Anyone who* wants to come is welcome.
	(b) He makes friends easily with ***whoever*** he meets.* He makes friends easily with *anyone who* he meets.
whatever	(c) He always says ***whatever*** comes into his mind. He always says *anything that* comes into his mind.
whenever	(d) You may leave ***whenever*** you wish. You may leave *at any time that* you wish.
wherever	(e) She can go ***wherever*** she wants to go. She can go *anyplace that* she wants to go.
however	(f) The students may dress ***however*** they please. The students may dress *in any way that* they please.

*In (b): **whomever** is also possible; it is the object of the verb **meets**. In American English, **whomever** is rare and very formal. In British English, **whoever** (not **whomever**) is used as the object form: *He makes friends easily with whoever he meets.*

Whenever it's too hot outside, I stay indoors.

Chapter 13
Adjective Clauses

13-1 Adjective Clause Pronouns Used as the Subject

I thanked the woman. **She** helped me. ↓ (a) I thanked the woman **who** helped me. (b) I thanked the woman **that** helped me.	In (a): ***I thanked the woman*** = a main clause; ***who helped me*** = an adjective clause.* An adjective clause modifies a noun. In (a): the adjective clause modifies ***woman***.
The book is mine. ***It*** is on the table. ↓ (c) The book **which** *is on the table* is mine. (d) The book **that** *is on the table* is mine.	In (a): ***who*** is the subject of the adjective clause. In (b): ***that*** is the subject of the adjective clause. NOTE: (a) and (b) have the same meaning; (c) and (d) have the same meaning.
	who = used for people ***which*** = used for things ***that*** = used for both people and things
(e) CORRECT: The book ***that is on the table*** is mine. (f) *INCORRECT:* The book is mine ~~that is on the table.~~	An adjective clause closely follows the noun it modifies.

*A *clause* is a structure that has a subject and a verb. There are two kinds of clauses: **independent** and **dependent**.
  In example (a):
  • The main clause (*I thanked the woman*) is also called an **independent** clause. An independent clause is a complete sentence and can stand alone.
  • The adjective clause (*who helped me*) is a **dependent** clause. A dependent clause is NOT a complete sentence and cannot stand alone. A dependent clause must be connected to an independent clause.

13-2　Adjective Clause Pronouns Used as the Object of a Verb

	The man was Mr. Jones.				
	I saw **him**.				
(a)	The man	**who(m)**	*I saw*	was Mr. Jones.	
(b)	The man	**that**	*I saw*	was Mr. Jones.	
(c)	The man	Ø	*I saw*	was Mr. Jones.	

Notice in the examples: The adjective clause pronouns are placed at the beginning of the clause.

In (a): **who** is usually used instead of **whom**, especially in speaking. **Whom** is generally used only in very formal English.

	The movie wasn't very good.			
	We saw **it** last night.			
(d)	The movie	**which**	*we saw last night*	wasn't very good.
(e)	The movie	**that**	*we saw last night*	wasn't very good.
(f)	The movie	Ø	*we saw last night*	wasn't very good.

In (c) and (f): An object pronoun is often omitted (Ø) from an adjective clause. (A subject pronoun, however, may not be omitted.)

who(m) = used for people
which = used for things
that = used for both people and things

(g)	*INCORRECT:*	The man who(m) I saw ~~him~~ was Mr. Jones.
		The man that I saw ~~him~~ was Mr. Jones.
		The man I saw ~~him~~ was Mr. Jones.

In (g): The pronoun **him** must be removed. It is unnecessary because *who(m), that,* or Ø functions as the object of the verb **saw**.

13-3　Adjective Clause Pronouns Used as the Object of a Preposition

	She is the woman.		
	I told you **about her**.		
(a)	She is the woman	**about whom**	*I told you.*
(b)	She is the woman	**who(m)**	*I told you* **about.**
(c)	She is the woman	**that**	*I told you* **about.**
(d)	She is the woman	Ø	*I told you* **about.**

In very formal English, the preposition comes at the beginning of the adjective clause, as in (a) and (e). Usually, however, in everyday usage, the preposition comes after the subject and verb of the adjective clause, as in the other examples.

	The music was good.				
	We listened **to it** last night.				
(e)	The music	**to which**	*we listened*	*last night*	was good.
(f)	The music	**which**	*we listened* **to**	*last night*	was good.
(g)	The music	**that**	*we listened* **to**	*last night*	was good.
(h)	The music	Ø	*we listened* **to**	*last night*	was good.

NOTE: If the preposition comes at the beginning of the adjective clause, only **whom** or **which** may be used. A preposition is never immediately followed by **that** or **who**.

INCORRECT:	She is the woman ~~about who~~ I told you.
INCORRECT:	The music ~~to that~~ we listened last night was good.

13-4 Using *Whose*

I know the man. ***His bicycle*** was stolen. ↓ (a) I know the man *whose bicycle was stolen*.	***Whose*** is used to show possession. It carries the same meaning as other possessive pronouns used as adjectives: *his, her, its,* and *their.* Like *his, her, its,* and *their,* ***whose*** is connected to a noun: his bicycle → whose bicycle her composition → whose composition
The student writes well. I read ***her composition.*** ↓ (b) The student *whose composition I read* writes well.	Both ***whose*** and the noun it is connected to are placed at the beginning of the adjective clause. ***Whose*** cannot be omitted.
(c) I worked at a ***company*** *whose employees* wanted to form a union.	***Whose*** usually modifies people, but it may also be used to modify things, as in (c).
(d) That's the boy *whose parents* you met. (e) That's the boy *who's* in my math class. (f) That's the boy *who's been living* at our house since his mother was arrested.*	***Whose*** and ***who's*** have the same pronunciation. ***Who's*** can mean ***who is***, as in (e), or ***who has***, as in (f).

*When ***has*** is a helping verb in the present perfect, it is usually contracted with ***who*** in speaking and sometimes in informal writing, as in (f).
When ***has*** is a main verb, it is NOT contracted with ***who***: *I know a man **who has** a cook.*

13-5 Using *Where* in Adjective Clauses

	The building is very old. He lives ***there*** (***in that building***).			***Where*** is used in an adjective clause to modify a place (*city, country, room, house,* etc.).
(a)	The building	*where*	*he lives*	is very old.
(b)	The building	*in which*	*he lives*	is very old.
	The building	*which*	*he lives in*	is very old.
	The building	*that*	*he lives in*	is very old.
	The building	Ø	*he lives in*	is very old.

If ***where*** is used, a preposition is NOT included in the adjective clause, as in (a).

If ***where*** is not used, the preposition must be included, as in (b).

13-6 Using *When* in Adjective Clauses

	I'll never forget the day. I met you ***then*** (***on that day***).			***When*** is used in an adjective clause to modify a noun of time (*year, day, time, century,* etc.).
(a)	I'll never forget the day	*when*	*I met you.*	
(b)	I'll never forget the day	*on which*	*I met you.*	
(c)	I'll never forget the day	*that*	*I met you.*	
(d)	I'll never forget the day	Ø	*I met you.*	

The use of a preposition in an adjective clause that modifies a noun of time is somewhat different from that in other adjective clauses: a preposition is used preceding ***which***, as in (b); otherwise, the preposition is omitted.

13-7 Using Adjective Clauses to Modify Pronouns

(a) There is **someone** *I want you to meet*. (b) **Everything** *he said* was pure nonsense. (c) **Anybody** *who wants to come* is welcome.	Adjective clauses can modify indefinite pronouns (e.g., *someone, everybody*). Object pronouns (e.g., *who(m), that, which*) are usually omitted in the adjective clause, as in (a) and (b).
(d) Paula was **the only one** *I knew at the party*. (e) Scholarships are available for **those** *who need financial assistance*.	Adjective clauses can modify **the one(s)** and **those**.*
(f) *INCORRECT:* ~~I who am a student at this school~~ come from a country in Asia. (g) It is *I who am responsible*. (h) **He** *who laughs last* laughs best.	Adjective clauses are almost never used to modify personal pronouns. Native English speakers would not write the sentence in (f). Example (g) is possible, but very formal and uncommon. Example (h) is a well-known saying in which **he** is used as an indefinite pronoun (meaning "anyone" or "any person").

*An adjective clause with **which** can also be used to modify the demonstrative pronoun **that**:
 We sometimes fear **that which** we do not understand.
 The bread my mother makes is much better than **that which** you can buy at a store.

Anyone *who wants to save money* can come to the circus on Wednesday.
Half-price tickets are available for **those** *who come* on Wednesday.

13-8 Punctuating Adjective Clauses

General guidelines for the punctuation of adjective clauses:
 (1) DO NOT USE COMMAS IF the adjective clause is necessary to identify the noun it modifies.*
 (2) USE COMMAS IF the adjective clause simply gives additional information and is not necessary to identify the noun it modifies.**

(a) *The professor* who teaches Chemistry 101 is an excellent lecturer.	In (a): No commas are used. The adjective clause is necessary to identify which professor is meant.
(b) *Professor Wilson,* who teaches Chemistry 101, is an excellent lecturer.	In (b): Commas are used. The adjective clause is not necessary to identify Professor Wilson. We already know who he is: he has a name. The adjective clause simply gives additional information.
(c) *Hawaii,* which consists of eight principal islands, is a favorite vacation spot.	GUIDELINE: Use commas, as in (b), (c), and (d), if an adjective clause modifies a proper noun. (A proper noun begins with a capital letter.)
(d) *Mrs. Smith,* who is a retired teacher, does volunteer work at the hospital.	NOTE: A comma reflects a pause in speech.
(e) *The man* $\begin{Bmatrix} who(m) \\ that \\ \emptyset \end{Bmatrix}$ *I met* teaches chemistry.	In (e): If no commas are used, any possible pronoun may be used in the adjective clause. Object pronouns may be omitted.
(f) *Mr. Lee,* whom I met yesterday, teaches chemistry.	In (f): When commas are necessary, the pronoun *that* may not be used (only *who, whom, which, whose, where,* and *when* may be used), and object pronouns cannot be omitted.
COMPARE THE MEANING: (g) We took some children on a picnic. *The children, who wanted to play soccer,* ran to an open field as soon as we arrived at the park. (h) We took some children on a picnic. *The children who wanted to play soccer* ran to an open field as soon as we arrived at the park. The others played a different game.	In (g): The use of commas means that *all* of the children wanted to play soccer and *all* of the children ran to an open field. The adjective clause is used only to give additional information about the children. In (h): The lack of commas means that *only some* of the children wanted to play soccer. The adjective clause is used to identify which children ran to the open field.

 *Adjective clauses that do not require commas are called *essential* or *restrictive* or *identifying.*

 **Adjective clauses that require commas are called *nonessential* or *nonrestrictive* or *nonidentifying.* NOTE: Nonessential adjective clauses are more common in writing than in speaking.

13-9 Using Expressions of Quantity in Adjective Clauses

In my class there are 20 students. *Most of **them*** are from Asia.	An adjective clause may contain an expression of quantity with ***of***: *some of, many of, most of, none of, two of, half of, both of,* etc.
(a) In my class there are 20 students, *most of **whom*** are from Asia.	
(b) He gave several reasons, *only a few of **which*** were valid.	The expression of quantity precedes the pronoun. Only ***whom, which,*** and ***whose*** are used in this pattern.
(c) The teachers discussed Jim, *one of **whose problems*** was poor study habits.	This pattern is more common in writing than speaking. Commas are used.

13-10 Using *Which* to Modify a Whole Sentence

(a) Tom was late. ***That*** surprised me. (b) Tom was late, *which surprised me.*	The pronouns ***that*** and ***this*** can refer to the idea of a whole sentence which comes before.
	In (a): The word ***that*** refers to the whole sentence ***Tom was late***.
(c) The elevator is out of order. ***This*** is too bad. (d) The elevator is out of order, *which is too bad.*	Similarly, an adjective clause with ***which*** may modify the idea of a whole sentence.
	In (b): The word ***which*** refers to the whole sentence ***Tom was late***.
	Using ***which*** to modify a whole sentence is informal and occurs most frequently in spoken English. This structure is generally not appropriate in formal writing. Whenever it is written, however, it is preceded by a comma to reflect a pause in speech.

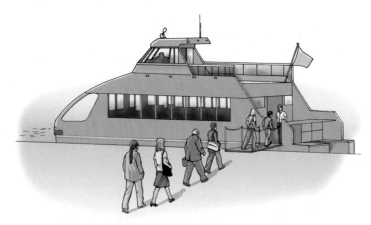

Some commuter ferries are passenger-only ferries,
which means that they don't carry vehicles.

13-11 Reducing Adjective Clauses to Adjective Phrases

CLAUSE: *A clause* is a group of related words that contains a subject and a verb.
PHRASE: *A phrase* is a group of related words that does not contain a subject and a verb.

(a) CLAUSE: The girl *who is sitting next to me* is Mai. (b) PHRASE: The girl *sitting next to me* is Mai. (c) CLAUSE: The girl (*whom*) *I saw* was Mai. (d) PHRASE: (*none*)	An adjective phrase is a reduction of an adjective clause. It modifies a noun. It does not contain a subject and verb. Examples (a) and (b) have the same meaning. Only adjective clauses that have a subject pronoun — *who*, *which*, or *that* — are reduced to modifying adjective phrases. The adjective clause in (c) cannot be reduced to an adjective phrase.

(e) CLAUSE: The man *who is talking* to John is from Korea.
  PHRASE: The man   Ø Ø *talking* to John is from Korea.
 	
(f) CLAUSE: The ideas *which are presented* in that book are good.
  PHRASE: The ideas   Ø   Ø   *presented* in that book are good.
 	
(g) CLAUSE: Ann is the woman *that is   responsible* for the error.
  PHRASE: Ann is the woman   Ø Ø *responsible* for the error.
	There are two ways in which an adjective clause is changed to an adjective phrase.
	
	1. If the adjective clause contains the *be* form of a verb, omit the subject pronoun and the *be* form, as in (e), (f), and (g).*

(h) CLAUSE: English has an alphabet *that consists* of 26 letters.
  PHRASE: English has an alphabet   Ø   *consisting* of 26 letters.
 	
(i) CLAUSE: Anyone *who wants   to come* with us is welcome.
  PHRASE: Anyone Ø *wanting* to come with us is welcome.
	2. If there is no *be* form of a verb in the adjective clause, it is sometimes possible to omit the subject pronoun and change the verb to its *-ing* form, as in (h) and (i).

(j) **Paris,** *which is the capital of France,* is an exciting city. (k) **Paris,** *the capital of France,* is an exciting city.	If the adjective clause requires commas, as in (j), the adjective phrase also requires commas, as in (k). An adjective phrase in which a noun follows another noun, as in (k), is called an *appositive*.

*If an adjective clause that contains *be* + *a single adjective* is changed, the adjective is moved to its normal position in front of the noun it modifies.

  CLAUSE: ***Fruit that is fresh*** *tastes better than old, soft, mushy fruit.*
  CORRECT PHRASE: ***Fresh fruit*** *tastes better than old, soft, mushy fruit.*
  INCORRECT PHRASE: *Fruit fresh tastes better than old, soft, mushy fruit.*

Chapter 14
Gerunds and Infinitives, Part 1

14-1 Gerunds: Introduction

(a) $\overline{Playing}^{\text{S}}$ tennis $\overline{is}^{\text{V}}$ fun.	A *gerund* is the *-ing* form of a verb used as a noun.* A gerund is used in the same ways as a noun, i.e., as a subject or as an object.
(b) $\overline{We}^{\text{S}}$ $\overline{enjoy}^{\text{V}}$ $\overline{playing}^{\text{O}}$ tennis.	In (a): *playing* is a gerund. It is used as the subject of the sentence. *Playing tennis* is a *gerund phrase*.
	In (b): *playing* is a gerund used as the object of the verb *enjoy*.
(c) He's excited $\overline{about}^{\text{PREP}}$ $\overline{playing}^{\text{O}}$ tennis.	In (c): *playing* is a gerund used as the object of the preposition *about*.

*Compare the uses of the *-ing* form of verbs:
    (1) ***Walking*** *is good exercise.* → ***walking*** = a gerund used as the subject of the sentence.
    (2) *Bob and Ann are* ***playing*** *tennis.* → ***playing*** = a present participle used as part of the present progressive tense.
    (3) *I heard some* ***surprising*** *news.* → ***surprising*** = a present participle used as an adjective.

Rita *enjoys* **playing** tennis when she has a good partner.

14-2 Using Gerunds as the Objects of Prepositions

(a) We talked *about going* to Canada for our vacation. (b) Sue is in charge *of organizing* the meeting. (c) I'm interested *in learning* more about your work.	A gerund is frequently used as the object of a preposition.
(d) I'*m used to sleeping* with the window open. (e) I'*m accustomed to sleeping** with the window open. (f) I *look forward to going* home next month.	In (d) through (f): *to* is a preposition, not part of an infinitive form, so a gerund follows.
(g) We *talked about not going* to the meeting, but finally decided we should go.	NEGATIVE FORM: *not* precedes a gerund.

Common preposition combinations followed by gerunds

be excited
be worried } *about doing* it

complain
dream
talk
think } *about/of doing* it

apologize
blame someone
forgive someone
have an excuse
have a reason
be responsible
thank someone } *for doing* it

keep someone
prevent someone
prohibit someone
stop someone } *from doing* it

be interested
believe
participate
succeed } *in doing it*

be accused
be capable
be guilty
instead
take advantage
take care } *of doing* it

be tired *of/from doing* it

insist *on doing* it

be accustomed
in addition
be committed
be devoted
look forward
object
be opposed
be used } *to doing* it

*Possible in British English: *I'm accustomed to sleep with the window open.*

14-3 Common Verbs Followed by Gerunds

verb + gerund (a) I *enjoy* *playing* tennis.	Gerunds are used as the objects of certain verbs. In (a): *enjoy* is followed by a gerund (*playing*). *Enjoy* is not followed by an infinitive. INCORRECT: I enjoy ~~to play~~ tennis. Common verbs that are followed by gerunds are listed below.
(b) Joe *quit smoking*. (c) Joe *gave up smoking*.	Examples (b) and (c) have the same meaning. Some phrasal verbs,* e.g., *give up*, are followed by gerunds. See these phrasal verbs in parentheses below.

Verb + *gerund*

enjoy	quit (give up)	avoid	consider
appreciate	finish (get through)	postpone (put off)	discuss
mind	stop**	delay	mention
		keep (keep on)	suggest

*A *phrasal verb* consists of a verb and a particle (a small word such as a preposition) that together have a special meaning. For example, *put off* means "postpone."

****Stop** can also be followed by an infinitive of purpose. *He **stopped** at the station (**in order**) **to get** some gas.* See *infinitives of purpose*, Charts 14-7, p. 80, and 15-1, p. 84.

14-4 *Go* + Gerund

(a) Did you *go shopping*? (b) We *went fishing* yesterday.	*Go* is followed by a gerund in certain idiomatic expressions to express, for the most part, recreational activities.

Go + gerund

go biking	go dancing	go running	go skiing
go birdwatching	go fishing*	go sailing	go skinnydipping
go boating	go hiking	go shopping	go sledding
go bowling	go hunting	go sightseeing	go snorkeling
go camping	go jogging	go skating	go swimming
go canoeing/kayaking	go mountain climbing	go skateboarding	go window shopping

*Also, in British English: *go angling*.

14-5 Special Expressions Followed by *-ing*

(a) We *had fun* We *had a good time* } *playing* volleyball.	*-ing* forms follow certain special expressions: **have fun/a good time** + **-ing** **have trouble/difficulty** + **-ing** **have a hard time/difficult time** + **-ing**
(b) I *had trouble* I *had difficulty* I *had a hard time* I *had a difficult time* } *finding* his house.	
(c) Sam *spends* most of his time *studying*. (d) I *waste a lot of time watching* TV.	**spend** + *expression of time or money* + **-ing** **waste** + *expression of time or money* + **-ing**
(e) She *sat at her desk writing* a letter. (f) I *stood there wondering* what to do next. (g) He *is lying in bed reading* a novel.	**sit** + *expression of place* + **-ing** **stand** + *expression of place* + **-ing** **lie** + *expression of place* + **-ing**
(h) When I walked into my office, I *found George using* my telephone. (i) When I walked into my office, I *caught a thief looking* through my desk drawers.	**find** + *(pro)noun* + **-ing** **catch** + *(pro)noun* + **-ing** In (h) and (i): Both *find* and *catch* mean "discover." *Catch* often expresses anger or displeasure.

Mrs. Garcia works in the city five days a week.
She *spends* a lot of time *commuting*.

14-6 Common Verbs Followed by Infinitives

Verb + Infinitive

(a) I *hope to see* you again soon.	An *infinitive* = *to* + *the simple form of a verb* (*to see, to be, to go, etc.*).
(b) He *promised to be* here by ten.	
	Some verbs are followed immediately by an infinitive, as in (a) and (b).
(c) He *promised not to be* late.	Negative form: ***not*** precedes the infinitive, as in (c).

Common verbs followed by infinitives

hope to (do something)	promise to	seem to	expect to
plan to	agree to	appear to	would like to
intend to*	offer to	pretend to	want to
decide to	refuse to	ask to	need to

Verb + Object + Infinitive

(d) Mr. Lee *told me to be* here at ten o'clock.	Some verbs are followed by a (pro)noun object and then an infinitive, as in (d) and (e).
(e) The police *ordered the driver to stop*.	
(f) I *was told to be* here at ten o'clock.	These verbs are followed immediately by an infinitive when they are used in the passive, as in (f) and (g).
(g) The driver *was ordered* to stop.	

Common verbs followed by (pro)nouns and infinitives

tell someone to	invite someone to	require someone to	expect someone to
advise someone to**	permit someone to	order someone to	would like someone to
encourage someone to	allow someone to	force someone to	want someone to
remind someone to	warn someone to	ask someone to	need someone to

Verb + Infinitive/Verb + Object + Infinitive

(h) I *expect to pass* the test.	Some verbs have two patterns:
(i) I *expect Mary to pass* the test.	• *verb* + *infinitive*, as in (h)
	• *verb* + *object* + infinitive, as in (i)
	COMPARE:
	In (h): I think I will pass the test.
	In (i): I think Mary will pass the test.

Common verbs followed by infinitives or by objects and then infinitives

ask to / ask someone to	want to / want someone to
expect to / expect someone to	would like to / would like someone to
need to / need someone to	

*****Intend** is usually followed by an infinitive (*I **intend to go** to the meeting.*) but sometimes may be followed by a gerund (*I **intend going** to the meeting.*) with no change in meaning.

****A gerund is used after ***advise*** (active) if there is no noun or pronoun object.

    COMPARE:

      (1) *He advised buying a Fiat.*

      (2) *He advised me to buy a Fiat. I was advised to buy a Fiat.*

14-7 Common Verbs Followed by Either Infinitives or Gerunds

Some verbs can be followed by either an infinitive or a gerund, sometimes with no difference in meaning, as in Group A below, and sometimes with a difference in meaning, as in Group B below.

Group A: Verb + Infinitive or Gerund, with No Difference in Meaning

begin like hate	The verbs in Group A may be followed by either an
start love can't stand	infinitive or a gerund with little or no difference in
continue prefer* can't bear	meaning.

(a) It *began to rain.* / It *began raining.*	In (a): There is no difference between **began to rain** and
(b) I *started to work.* / I *started working.*	**began raining**.
(c) It *was beginning to rain.*	If the main verb is progressive, an infinitive (not a gerund) is usually used, as in (c).

Group B: Verb + Infinitive or Gerund, with a Difference in Meaning

remember regret stop	The verbs in Group B may be followed by either an
forget try	infinitive or a gerund, but the meaning is different.

(d) Judy always *remembers to lock* the door.	**Remember** + *infinitive* = remember to perform responsibility, duty, or task, as in (d).
(e) Sam often *forgets to lock* the door.	**Forget** + *infinitive* = forget to perform a responsibility, duty, or task, as in (e).
(f) I *remember seeing* the Alps for the first time. The sight was impressive.	**Remember** + *gerund* = remember (recall) something that happened in the past, as in (f).
(g) I*'ll never forget seeing* the Alps for the first time.	**Forget** + *gerund* = forget something that happened in the past, as in (g).**
(h) I *regret to tell* you that you failed the test.	**Regret** + *infinitive* = regret to say, to tell someone, to inform someone of some bad news, as in (h).
(i) I *regret lending* him some money. He never paid me back.	**Regret** + *gerund* = regret something that happened in the past, as in (i).
(j) I*'m trying to learn* English.	**Try** + *infinitive* = make an effort, as in (j).
(k) The room was hot. I *tried opening* the window, but that didn't help. So I *tried turning* on the fan, but I was still hot. Finally, I turned on the air conditioner.	**Try** + *gerund* = experiment with a new or different approach to see if it works, as in (k).
(l) The students *stopped talking* when the professor entered the room. The room became quiet.	**Stop** + *gerund* = stop an activity.
(m) When Ann saw her professor in the hallway, she *stopped (in order) to talk* to him.	**Stop** can also be followed immediately by an infinitive of purpose, as in (m): Ann stopped walking in order to talk to her professor. (See Chart 15-1, p. 84.)

*Notice the patterns with **prefer:**
    prefer + *gerund: I **prefer staying** home **to going** to the concert.*
    prefer + *infinitive: I'd **prefer to stay** home (rather) **than (to) go** to the concert.*

Forget followed by a gerund usually occurs in a negative sentence or in a question: e.g., *I'll never forget, I can't forget, Have you ever forgotten,* and *Can you ever forget* are often followed by a gerund phrase.

14-8 *It* + Infinitive; Gerunds and Infinitives as Subjects

(a) *It* is difficult *to learn* a second language.	Often an infinitive phrase is used with *it* as the subject of a sentence. The word *it* refers to and has the same meaning as the infinitive phrase at the end of the sentence. In (a): *It* means "to learn a second language."
(b) *Learning* a second language is difficult.	A gerund phrase is frequently used as the subject of a sentence, as in (b).
(c) *To learn* a second language is difficult.	An infinitive can also be used as the subject of a sentence, as in (c), but far more commonly an infinitive phrase is used with *it*, as in (a).
(d) It is easy *for young children* to learn a second language. *Learning* a second language is easy *for young children*. *To learn* a second language is easy *for young children*.	The phrase *for (someone)* may be used to specify exactly who the speaker is talking about, as in (d).

Washing the dishes is George's job when his wife has to work on Saturdays.

14-9 Reference List of Verbs Followed by Gerunds

Verbs with a bullet (•) can also be followed by infinitives. See Chart 14-10.

1.	admit	He *admitted stealing* the money.
2.	advise•	She *advised waiting* until tomorrow.
3.	anticipate	I *anticipate having* a good time on vacation.
4.	appreciate	I *appreciated hearing* from them.
5.	avoid	He *avoided answering* my question.
6.	can't bear•	I *can't bear waiting* in long lines.
7.	begin•	It *began raining*.
8.	complete	I finally *completed writing* my term paper.
9.	consider	I *will consider going* with you.
10.	continue•	He *continued speaking*.
11.	delay	He *delayed leaving* for school.
12.	deny	She *denied committing* the crime.
13.	discuss	They *discussed opening* a new business.
14.	dislike	I *dislike driving* long distances.
15.	enjoy	We *enjoyed visiting* them.
16.	finish	She *finished studying* about ten.
17.	forget•	I*'ll never forget visiting* Napoleon's tomb.
18.	hate•	I *hate making* silly mistakes.
19.	can't help	I *can't help worrying* about it.
20.	keep	I *keep hoping* he will come.
21.	like•	I *like going* to movies.
22.	love•	I *love going* to operas.
23.	mention	She *mentioned going* to a movie.
24.	mind	*Would* you *mind helping* me with this?
25.	miss	I *miss being* with my family.
26.	postpone	Let's *postpone leaving* until tomorrow.
27.	practice	The athlete *practiced throwing* the ball.
28.	prefer•	Ann *prefers walking* to driving to work.
29.	quit	He *quit trying* to solve the problem.
30.	recall	I *don't recall meeting* him before.
31.	recollect	I *don't recollect meeting* him before.
32.	recommend	She *recommended seeing* the show.
33.	regret•	I *regret telling* him my secret.
34.	remember•	I *can remember meeting* him when I was a child.
35.	resent	I *resent her interfering* in my business.
36.	resist	I *couldn't resist eating* the dessert.
37.	risk	She *risks losing* all of her money.
38.	can't stand•	I *can't stand waiting* in long lines.
39.	start•	It *started raining*.
40.	stop	She *stopped going* to classes when she got sick.
41.	suggest	She *suggested going* to a movie.
42.	tolerate	She *won't tolerate cheating* during an examination.
43.	try•	I *tried changing* the light bulb, but the lamp still didn't work.
44.	understand	I *don't understand his leaving* school.

14-10 Reference List of Verbs Followed by Infinitives

Verbs with a bullet (•) can also be followed by gerunds. See Chart 14-9.

Verbs Followed Immediately by an Infinitive

1.	afford	I *can't afford to buy* it.
2.	agree	They *agreed to help* us.
3.	appear	She *appears to be* tired.
4.	arrange	I*'ll arrange to meet* you at the airport.
5.	ask	He *asked to come* with us.
6.	can't bear•	I *can't bear to wait* in long lines.
7.	beg	He *begged to come* with us.
8.	begin•	It *began to rain.*
9.	care	I *don't care to see* that show.
10.	claim	She *claims to know* a famous movie star.
11.	consent	She finally *consented to marry* him.
12.	continue•	He *continued to speak.*
13.	decide	I *have decided to leave* on Monday.
14.	demand	I *demand to know* who is responsible.
15.	deserve	She *deserves to win* the prize.
16.	expect	I *expect to enter* graduate school in the fall.
17.	fail	She *failed to return* the book to the library on time.
18.	forget•	I *forgot to mail* the letter.
19.	hate•	I *hate to make* silly mistakes.
20.	hesitate	*Don't hesitate to ask* for my help.
21.	hope	Jack *hopes to arrive* next week.
22.	intend	He *intends to be* a firefighter.
23.	learn	He *learned to play* the piano.
24.	like•	I *like to go* to the movies.
25.	love•	I *love to go* to operas.
26.	manage	She *managed to finish* her work early.
27.	mean	I *didn't mean to hurt* your feelings.
28.	need	I *need to have* your opinion.
29.	offer	They *offered to help* us.
30.	plan	I*'m planning to have* a party.
31.	prefer•	Ann *prefers to walk* to work.
32.	prepare	We *prepared to welcome* them.
33.	pretend	He *pretends not to understand.*
34.	promise	I *promise not to be* late.
35.	refuse	I *refuse to believe* his story.
36.	regret•	I *regret to tell* you that you failed.
37.	remember•	I *remembered to lock* the door.
38.	seem	That cat *seems to be* friendly.
39.	can't stand•	I *can't stand to wait* in long lines.
40.	start•	It *started to rain.*
41.	struggle	I *struggled to stay* awake.
42.	swear	She *swore to tell* the truth.
43.	talk	He *tends to talk* too much.
44.	threaten	She *threatened to tell* my parents.
45.	try•	I*'m trying to learn* English.
46.	volunteer	He *volunteered to help* us.
47.	wait	I*'ll wait to hear* from you.
48.	want	I *want to tell* you something.
49.	wish	She *wishes to come* with us.

Verbs Followed by a (Pro)noun + an Infinitive

50.	advise•	She *advised me to wait* until tomorrow.
51.	allow	She *allowed me to use* her car.
52.	ask	I *asked John to help* us.
53.	beg	They *begged us to come.*
54.	cause	Her laziness *caused her to fail.*
55.	challenge	She *challenged me to race* her to the corner.
56.	convince	I couldn't *convince him to accept* our help.
57.	dare	He *dared me to do* better than he had done.
58.	encourage	He *encouraged me to try* again.
59.	expect	I *expect you to be* on time.
60.	forbid	I *forbid you to tell* him.
61.	force	They *forced him to tell* the truth.
62.	hire	She *hired a boy to mow* the lawn.
63.	instruct	He *instructed them to be* careful.
64.	invite	Harry *invited the Johnsons to come* to his party.
65.	need	We *needed Chris to help* us figure out the solution.
66.	order	The judge *ordered me to pay* a fine.
67.	permit	He *permitted the children to stay* up late.
68.	persuade	I *persuaded him to come* for a visit.
69.	remind	She *reminded me to lock* the door.
70.	require	Our teacher *requires us to be* on time.
71.	teach	My brother *taught me to swim.*
72.	tell	The doctor *told me to take* these pills.
73.	urge	I *urged her to apply* for the job.
74.	want	I *want you to be* happy.
75.	warn	I *warned you not to drive* too fast.

Chapter 15
Gerunds and Infinitives, Part 2

15-1 Infinitive of Purpose: *In Order To*

(a) He came here *in order to study* English.	*In order to* is used to express *purpose*. It answers the question "Why?" *In order* is often omitted, as in (b).
(b) He came here *to study* English.	
(c) INCORRECT: He came here ~~for studying~~ English. (d) INCORRECT: He came here ~~for to study~~ English. (e) INCORRECT: He came here ~~for study~~ English.	To express purpose, use (*in order*) *to*, not *for*, with a verb.*
(f) I went to the store *for some bread*.	*For* can be used to express purpose, but it is a preposition and is followed by a noun object, as in (f).
(g) I went to the store *to buy* some bread.	

*Exception: The phrase *be used for* expresses the typical or general purpose of a thing. In this case, the preposition *for* is followed by a gerund: *A saw is used for cutting wood.* Also possible: *A saw is used to cut wood.*

    However, to talk about a particular thing and a particular situation, *be used* + *an infinitive* is used: *A chain saw was used to cut* (NOT *for cutting*) *down the old oak tree.*

15-2 Adjectives Followed by Infinitives

(a) We *were* **sorry to** *hear* the bad news.	Certain adjectives can be immediately followed by infinitives, as in (a) and (b).
(b) I *was* **surprised to** *see* Ted at the meeting.	In general, these adjectives describe a person (or persons), not a thing. Many of these adjectives describe a person's feelings or attitudes.

Common adjectives followed by infinitives

glad to (do it)	sorry to*	ready to	careful to	surprised to*
happy to	sad to*	prepared to	hesitant to	amazed to*
pleased to	upset to*	anxious to	reluctant to	astonished to*
delighted to	disappointed to*	eager to	afraid to	shocked to*
content to		willing to		stunned to*
relieved to	embarrassed to	motivated to	certain to	
lucky to	proud to	determined to	likely to	
fortunate to	ashamed to		unlikely to	

*The expressions with asterisks are usually followed by infinitive phrases with verbs such as *see, learn, discover, find out, hear.*

15-3 Using Infinitives with *Too* and *Enough*

COMPARE: (a) That box is *too heavy* for Bob to lift. (b) That box is *very heavy*, but Bob can lift it.	In the speaker's mind, the use of *too* implies a negative result. In (a): *too heavy* = It is *impossible* for Bob to lift that box. In (b): *very heavy* = It is *possible but difficult* for Bob to lift that box.
(c) I am *strong enough* *to lift* that box. I can lift it. (d) I have *enough strength* *to lift* that box. (e) I have *strength enough* *to lift* that box.	*Enough* follows an adjective, as in (c). Usually *enough* precedes a noun, as in (d). In formal English, it may follow a noun, as in (e).

15-4 Passive Infinitives and Gerunds

(a) I didn't *expect to be asked* to his party.	PASSIVE INFINITIVE: *to be* + *past participle* In (a): *to be asked* is a passive infinitive. The understood *by*-phrase is *by him*: *I didn't expect to be asked to his party (by him)*.
(b) I enjoyed *being asked* to his party.	PASSIVE GERUND: *being* + *past participle* In (b): *being asked* is a passive gerund. The understood *by*-phrase is *by him*: *I enjoyed being asked to his party (by him)*.

15-5 Using Gerunds or Passive Infinitives Following *Need*

(a) I *need to paint* my house. (b) John *needs to be told* the truth.	Usually an infinitive follows *need*, as in (a) and (b).
(c) My house *needs painting*. (d) My house *needs to be painted*.	In certain circumstances, a gerund may follow *need*, as in (c). In this case, the gerund carries a passive meaning. Usually the situations involve fixing or improving something. Examples (c) and (d) have the same meaning.

15-6 Using Verbs of Perception

(a) I *saw* my friend *run* down the street.	Certain verbs of perception are followed by either *the simple form** or the *-ing* form**** of a verb.
(b) I *saw* my friend *running* down the street.	
(c) I *heard* the rain *fall* on the roof.	Examples (a) and (b) have essentially the same meaning, except that the *-ing* form emphasizes the idea of "while." In (b): I saw my friend while she was running down the street.
(d) I *heard* the rain *falling* on the roof.	
(e) When I walked into the apartment, I *heard* my roommate *singing* in the shower.	Sometimes (not always) there is a clear difference between using the simple form or the *-ing* form.
(f) I *heard* a famous opera star *sing* at the concert last night.	The use of the *-ing* form gives the idea that an activity is already in progress when it is perceived, as in (e): The singing was in progress when I first heard it.
	In (f): I heard the singing from beginning to end. It was not in progress when I first heard it.

Verbs of perception followed by the simple form or the *-ing* form

see	look at	hear	feel	smell
notice	observe	listen to		
watch				

The simple form of a verb = the infinitive form without *to*. INCORRECT: I saw my friend ~~to~~ run down the street.

**The *-ing* form refers to the present participle.

15-7 Using the Simple Form after *Let* and *Help*

(a) My father *lets* me *drive* his car.	*Let* is followed by the simple form of a verb, not an infinitive.
(b) I *let* my friend *borrow* my bicycle.	INCORRECT: My father lets me ~~to~~ drive his car.
(c) *Let's go* to a movie.	
(d) My brother *helped* me *wash* my car.	*Help* is often followed by the simple form of a verb, as in (d).
(e) My brother *helped* me *to wash* my car.	Although less common, an infinitive is also possible, as in (e).
	Both (d) and (e) are correct.

15-8 Using Causative Verbs: *Make, Have, Get*

(a) I *made* my brother *carry* my suitcase. (b) I *had* my brother *carry* my suitcase. (c) I *got* my brother *to carry* my suitcase.	*Make*, *have*, and *get* can be used to express the idea that "X" causes "Y" to do something. When they are used as causative verbs, their meanings are similar but not identical. In (a): My brother had no choice. I insisted that he carry my suitcase. In (b): My brother carried my suitcase because I asked him to. In (c): I managed to persuade my brother to carry my suitcase.
Forms X **makes** Y **do** something. (*simple form*) X **has** Y **do** something. (*simple form*) X **gets** Y **to do** something. (*infinitive*)	

Causative *Make*

(d) Mrs. Lee *made* her son *clean* his room. (e) Sad movies *make* me *cry*.	Causative *make* is followed by the simple form of a verb, not an infinitive. *INCORRECT*: She made him ~~to~~ clean his room. **Make** gives the idea that "X" **gives** "Y" **no choice**. In (d): Mrs. Lee's son had no choice.

Causative *Have*

(f) I *had* the plumber *repair* the leak. (g) Jane *had* the waiter *bring* her some tea.	Causative *have* is followed by the simple form of a verb, not an infinitive. *INCORRECT*: I had him ~~to~~ repair the leak. **Have** gives the idea that "X" **requests** "Y" to do something. In (f): The plumber repaired the leak because I asked him to.

Causative *Get*

(h) The students *got* the teacher *to dismiss* class early. (i) Jack *got* his friends *to play* soccer with him after school.	Causative *get* is followed by an infinitive. **Get** gives the idea that "X" **persuades** "Y" to do something. In (h): The students managed to persuade the teacher to let them leave early.

Passive Causatives

(j) I *had* my watch *repaired* (by someone). (k) I *got* my watch *repaired* (by someone).	The past participle is used after **have** and **get** to give a passive meaning. In this case, there is usually little or no difference in meaning between **have** and **get**. In (j) and (k): I caused my watch to be repaired by someone.

Chapter 16
Coordinating Conjunctions

16-1 Parallel Structure

One use of a conjunction is to connect words or phrases that have the same grammatical function in a sentence. This use of conjunctions is called "parallel structure." The conjunctions used in this pattern are **and, but, or**, and **nor**. These words are called "coordinating conjunctions."

(a) *Steve **and** his friend* are coming to dinner.	In (a): *noun* + **and** + *noun*
(b) Susan *raised* her hand **and** *snapped* her fingers.	In (b): *verb* + **and** + *verb*
(c) He *is waving* his arms **and** (*is*) *shouting* at us.	In (c): *verb* + **and** + *verb* (The second auxiliary may be omitted if it is the same as the first auxiliary.)
(d) These shoes are *old* **but** *comfortable*.	In (d): *adjective* + **but** + *adjective*
(e) He wants *to watch* TV **or** (*to*) *listen* to some music.	In (e): *infinitive* + **or** + *infinitive* (The second *to* is usually omitted.)

16-2 Parallel Structure: Using Commas

(a) **Steve** and **Joe** are in class.	No commas are used when *and* connects **two** parts of a parallel structure, as in (a).
(b) *INCORRECT PUNCTUATION:* Steve, and Joe are in class.	
(c) **Steve, Joe** and **Rita** are in class.	When *and* connects **three or more** parts of a parallel structure, a comma is used between the first items in the series.
(d) **Steve, Joe,** and **Rita** are in class.	A comma may also be used before *and,* as in (d) and (f). The use of this comma is optional (i.e., the writer can choose).*
(e) **Steve, Joe, Rita, Jan** and **Kim** are in class.	NOTE: A comma often represents a pause in speech.
(f) **Steve, Joe, Rita, Jan,** and **Kim** are in class.	

*The purpose of punctuation is to make writing clear for readers. This chart and others in this chapter describe the usual use of commas in parallel structures. Sometimes commas are required according to convention (i.e., the expected use by educated language users). Sometimes use of commas is a stylistic choice made by the experienced writer.

16-3 Paired Conjunctions: *Both . . . And; Not Only . . . But Also; Either . . . Or; Neither . . . Nor*

(a) **Both** my mother **and** my sister **are** here.	Two subjects connected by **both . . . and** take a plural verb, as in (a).
(b) **Not only** my mother **but also** my sister **is** here. (c) **Not only** my sister **but also** my parents **are** here. (d) **Neither** my mother **nor** my sister **is** here. (e) **Neither** my sister **nor** my parents **are** here.	When two subjects are connected by **not only . . . but also**, **either . . . or**, or **neither . . . nor**, the subject that is closer to the verb determines whether the verb is singular or plural.
(f) The research project will take **both** time **and** money. (g) Sue saw **not only** a fox in the woods **but (also)** a bear. (h) I'll take **either** chemistry **or** physics next quarter. (i) That book is **neither** interesting **nor** accurate.	Notice the parallel structure in the examples. The same grammatical form should follow each part of the paired conjunctions.*
	In (f): **both** + noun + **and** + noun In (g): **not only** + noun + **but also** + noun In (h): **either** + noun + **or** + noun In (i): **neither** + adjective + **nor** + adjective NOTE: Paired conjuctions are usually used for emphasis; they draw attention to both parts of the parallel structure.

*Paired conjunctions are also called "correlative conjunctions."

16-4 Separating Independent Clauses with Periods; Connecting Them with *And* and *But*

(a) It was raining hard. There was a strong wind.	Example (a) contains two *independent clauses* (i.e., two complete sentences).
(b) *INCORRECT PUNCTUATION:* It was raining hard, there was a strong wind.	PUNCTUATION: A period,* NOT A COMMA, is used to separate two independent clauses. The punctuation error in (b) is called a "run-on sentence." In spoken English, a pause, slightly longer than a pause for a comma, separates the two sentences.
(c) It was raining hard, *and* there was a strong wind. (d) It was raining hard. *And* there was a strong wind. (e) It was raining hard *and* there was a strong wind. (f) It was late, *but* he didn't care. (g) It was late. *But* he didn't care.	*And* and *but* (coordinating conjunctions) are often used to connect two independent clauses. PUNCTUATION: Usually a comma immediately precedes the conjunction, as in (c) and (f). In informal writing, a writer might choose to begin a sentence with a conjunction, as in (d) and (g). In a very short sentence, a writer might choose to omit the comma in front of *and*, as in (e). (Omitting the comma in front of *but* is rare.)

*In British English, a period is called a "full stop."

Chapter 17
Adverb Clauses

17-1 Introduction

Adverb clauses are used to show relationships between ideas. They show relationships of *time, cause and effect, contrast,* and *condition*.

<table>
<tr>
<td>

    adverb clause   main clause

(a) *When the phone rang,* the baby woke up.

(b) The baby woke up *when the phone rang*.
</td>
<td>
In (a) and (b): **when the phone rang** is an adverb clause of time. Examples (a) and (b) have the same meaning.

PUNCTUATION:
When an adverb clause precedes a main clause, as in (a), a comma is used to separate the clauses.
When the adverb clause follows, as in (b), usually no comma is used.
</td>
</tr>
<tr>
<td>
(c) *Because he was sleepy,* he went to bed.

(d) He went to bed *because he was sleepy*.
</td>
<td>
In (c) and (d), **because** introduces an adverb clause that shows a cause-and-effect relationship.
</td>
</tr>
<tr>
<td>
(e) *INCORRECT PUNCTUATION:*
  When we were in New York. We saw several plays.

(f) *INCORRECT PUNCTUATION:*
He went to bed. Because he was sleepy.
</td>
<td>
Adverb clauses are dependent clauses. They cannot stand alone as a sentence in written English. They must be connected to a main (or independent) clause.*
</td>
</tr>
</table>

Summary list of words used to introduce adverb clauses**

TIME		CAUSE AND EFFECT	CONTRAST	CONDITION
after	by the time (that)	because	even though	if
before	once	now that	although	unless
when	as/so long as	since	though	only if
while	whenever			whether or not
as	every time (that)		DIRECT CONTRAST	even if
as soon as	the first time (that)		while	in case
since	the last time (that)			
until	the next time (that)			

*See Chart 13-1, p. 69, for the definition of dependent and independent clauses.

**Words that introduce adverb clauses are called "subordinating conjunctions."

17-2 Using Adverb Clauses to Show Time Relationships

after *	(a) **After** *she graduates,* she will get a job. (b) **After** *she (had) graduated,* she got a job.	A present tense, NOT a future tense, is used in an adverb clause of time, as in (a) and (c) (See Chart 4-3, p. 22, for tense usage in future time clauses.)
before *	(c) I will leave **before** *he comes.* (d) I (had) left **before** *he came.*	
when	(e) **When** *I arrived,* he *was talking* on the phone. (f) **When** *I got there,* he *had* already *left.* (g) **When** *it began to rain,* I *stood* under a tree. (h) **When** *I was in Chicago,* I *visited* the museums. (i) **When** *I see him tomorrow,* I *will ask* him.	**when** = *at that time* Notice the different time relationships expressed by the tenses.
while as	(j) **While** *I was walking home,* it began to rain. (k) **As** *I was walking home,* it began to rain.	**while, as** = *during that time*
by the time	(l) **By the time** *he arrived,* we *had* already *left.* (m) **By the time** *he comes,* we *will have* already *left.*	**by the time** = *one event is completed before another event* Notice the use of the past perfect and future perfect in the main clause.
since	(n) I *haven't seen* him **since** *he left this morning.* (o) I *'ve known* her **ever since** *I was a child.*	**since** = *from that time to the present* In (o): *ever* adds emphasis. NOTE: The present perfect is used in the main clause.
until till	(p) We stayed there **until** *we finished our work.* (q) We stayed there **till** *we finished our work.*	**until, till** = *to that time and then no longer* (**Till** is used more in speaking than in writing; it is generally not used in formal English.)
as soon as once	(r) **As soon as** *it stops raining,* we will leave. (s) **Once** *it stops raining,* we will leave.	**as soon as, once** = *when one event happens, another event happens soon afterward*
as long as so long as	(t) I will never speak to him again **as long as** *I live.* (u) I will never speak to him again **so long as** *I live.*	**as long as, so long as** = *during all that time, from beginning to end*
whenever every time	(v) **Whenever** *I see her,* I say hello. (w) **Every time** *I see her,* I say hello.	**whenever** = *every time*
the first time the last time the next time	(x) **The first time** *(that) I went to New York,* I went to an opera. (y) I saw two plays **the last time** *(that) I went to New York.* (z) **The next time** *(that) I go to New York,* I'm going to see a ballet.	Adverb clauses can be introduced by: the { **first** / **second** / **third**, etc. / **last** / **next** / **etc.** } **time** (*that*)

*After and *before* are commonly used in the following expressions:

shortly *after*	**shortly** *before*
a short time *after*	**a short time** *before*
a little while *after*	**a little while** *before*
not long *after*	**not long** *before*
soon *after*	

17-3 Using Adverb Clauses to Show Cause and Effect

because	(a) **Because** he was sleepy, he went to bed. (b) He went to bed **because** he was sleepy.	An adverb clause may precede or follow the independent clause. Notice the punctuation in (a) and (b).
now that	(c) **Now that** I've finished the semester, I'm going to rest a few days and then take a trip. (d) Jack lost his job. **Now that** he's unemployed, he can't pay his bills.	**Now that** means "because now." In (c): **Now that I've finished the semester** means "because the semester is now over." **Now that** is used for present causes of present or future situations.
since	(e) **Since** Monday is a holiday, we don't have to go to work. (f) **Since** you're a good cook and I'm not, you should cook the dinner.	When **since** is used to mean "because," it expresses a known cause; it means "because it is a fact that" or "given that it is true that." Cause-and-effect sentences with **since** say, "Given the fact that X is true, Y is the result." In (e): "Given the fact that Monday is a holiday, we don't have to go to work."
	(g) **Since** I came here, I have met many people.	NOTE: **Since** has two meanings. One is "because." It is also used in time clauses, as in (g). See Chart 17-2.

17-4 Expressing Contrast (Unexpected Result): Using *Even Though*

(a) **Because** the weather was cold, I *didn't go* swimming. (b) **Even though** the weather was cold, I *went* swimming. (c) **Because** I wasn't tired, I *didn't go* to bed. (d) **Even though** I wasn't tired, I *went* to bed.	**Because** is used to express expected results. **Even though** is used to express unexpected results.* NOTE: Like **because**, **even though** introduces an adverb clause.

*Although and *though* have basically the same meaning and use as *even though*. See Chart 19-6, p. 102, for information on the use of *although* and *though*.

17-5 Showing Direct Contrast: *While*

(a) Mary is rich, **while** *John is poor.* (b) John is poor, **while** *Mary is rich.* (c) **While** *John is poor,* Mary is rich. (d) **While** *Mary is rich,* John is poor.	**While** is used to show direct contrast: "this" is exactly the opposite of "that."* Examples (a), (b), (c), and (d) all have the same meaning. Note the use of the comma in (a) and (b): In using **while** for direct contrast, a comma is often used even if the *while*-clause comes second (unlike the punctuation of most other adverb clauses).
COMPARE: (e) The phone rang **while** *I was studying.*	REMINDER: **While** is also used in time clauses and means "during that time," as in (e). See Chart 17-2.

*Whereas can have the same meaning and use as **while**, but it occurs mostly in formal written English and occurs with considerably less frequency than **while**: *Mary is rich, **whereas** John is poor.*

17-6 Expressing Conditions in Adverb Clauses: *If*-Clauses

(a) *If* it *rains* tomorrow, I *will take* my umbrella.	*If*-clauses (also called "adverb clauses of condition") present possible conditions. The main clause expresses RESULTS. In (a): POSSIBLE CONDITION = *it may rain tomorrow* RESULT = *I will take my umbrella* A present tense, not a future tense, is used in an *if*-clause even though the verb in the *if*-clause may refer to a future event or situation, as in (a).*

Words that introduce adverb clauses of condition (*if*-clauses)

if	even if	unless
whether or not	in case	only if

*See Chapter 20 for uses of other verb forms in sentences with *if*-clauses.

17-7 Shortened *If*-Clauses

(a) Are you a student? *If so* / *If you are*, the ticket is half-price. *If not* / *If you aren't*, the ticket is full price. (b) It's a popular concert. Do you have a ticket? *If so* / *If you do*, you're lucky. *If not* / *If you don't*, you're out of luck.	When an *if*-clause refers to the idea in the sentence immediately before it, it is sometimes shortened. In (a): *If so* / *If you are* = *If you are a student* *If not* / *If you aren't* = *If you aren't a student* In (b): *If so* / *If you do* = *If you have a ticket* *If not* / *If you don't* = *If you don't have a ticket*

17-8 Adverb Clauses of Condition: Using *Whether Or Not* and *Even If*

Whether or not

(a) I'm going to go swimming tomorrow *whether or not it is cold*. OR *whether it is cold or not*.	*Whether or not* expresses the idea that neither this condition nor that condition matters; the result will be the same. In (a): "If it is cold, I'm going swimming. If it is not cold, I'm going swimming. I don't care about the temperature. It doesn't matter."

Even if

(b) I have decided to go swimming tomorrow. *Even if the weather is cold*, I'm going to go swimming.	Sentences with *even if* are close in meaning to those with *whether or not*. *Even if* gives the idea that a particular condition does not matter. The result will not change.

17-9 Adverb Clauses of Condition: Using *In Case*

(a) I'll be at my uncle's house *in case* you *(should) need to reach me.*	*In case* expresses the idea that something probably won't happen, but it might. *In case* means "if by chance this should happen." NOTE: Using **should** in an adverb clause emphasizes the speaker's uncertainty that something will happen.

17-10 Adverb Clauses of Condition: Using *Unless*

(a) I'll go swimming tomorrow *unless* it's cold. (b) I'll go swimming tomorrow *if* it isn't cold.	**unless** = *if . . . not* In (a): *unless it's cold* means "if it isn't cold." Examples (a) and (b) have the same meaning.

17-11 Adverb Clauses of Condition: Using *Only If*

(a) The picnic will be canceled *only if* it rains. 　　If it's windy, we'll go on the picnic. 　　If it's cold, we'll go on the picnic. 　　If it's damp and foggy, we'll go on the picnic. 　　If it's unbearably hot, we'll go on the picnic.	**Only if** expresses the idea that there is only one condition that will cause a particular result.
(b) **Only if** it rains **will** the picnic **be canceled**.	When **only if** begins a sentence, the subject and verb of the main clause are inverted, as in (b).* No commas are used.

*Other subordinating conjunctions and prepositional phrases preceded by **only** at the beginning of a sentence require subject-verb inversion in the main clause:

　　Only when the teacher dismisses us **can we stand** and **leave** the room.
　　Only after the phone rang **did I realize** that I had fallen asleep in my chair.
　　Only in my hometown **do I feel** at ease.

Chapter 18

Reduction of Adverb Clauses to Modifying Adverbial Phrases

18-1 Introduction

(a)	Adverb clause:	*While **I** was **walking*** to class, I ran into an old friend.	In Chapter 13, we discussed changing adjective clauses to modifying phrases. (See Chart 13-11, p. 75.) Some adverb clauses may also be changed to modifying phrases, and the ways in which the changes are made are the same: • If there is a **be** form of the verb, omit the subject of the dependent clause and **be** verb, as in (b). OR • If there is no **be** form of a verb, omit the subject and change the verb to **-ing**, as in (d).
(b)	Modifying phrase:	*While **walking*** to class, I ran into an old friend.	
(c)	Adverb clause:	*Before **I left** for work,* I ate breakfast.	
(d)	Modifying phrase:	*Before **leaving** for work,* I ate breakfast.	
(e)	Change possible:	*While **I** was sitting in class, **I** fell asleep.* *While sitting in class, **I** fell asleep.*	An adverb clause can be changed to a modifying phrase **only when the subject of the adverb clause and the subject of the main clause are the same**. A *modifying adverbial phrase* that is the reduction of an adverb clause *modifies the subject* of the main clause.
(f)	Change possible:	*While **Ann** was sitting in class, **she** fell asleep.* (clause) *While sitting in class, **Ann** fell asleep.*	
(g)	No change possible:	*While **the teacher** was lecturing to the class, **I** fell asleep.**	No reduction (i.e., change) is possible if the subjects of the adverb clause and the main clause are different, as in (g).
(h)	*INCORRECT:*	~~While watching TV last night,~~ the phone rang.	In (h): *While watching* is called a "dangling modifier" or a "dangling participle," i.e., a modifier that is incorrectly "hanging alone" without an appropriate noun or pronoun subject to modify.

**While lecturing to the class, I fell asleep* means "While *I* was lecturing to the class, *I* fell asleep."

18-2 Changing Time Clauses to Modifying Adverbial Phrases

(a)	Clause:	**Since Maria came** to this country, she has made many friends.
(b)	Phrase:	**Since coming** to this country, Maria has made many friends.

Adverb clauses beginning with **after**, **before**, **while**, and **since** can be changed to modifying adverbial phrases.

(c)	Clause:	**After he (had) finished** his homework, Peter went to bed.
(d)	Phrase:	**After finishing** his homework, Peter went to bed.
(e)	Phrase:	**After having finished** his homework, Peter went to bed.

In (c): There is no difference in meaning between *After he finished* and *After he had finished*. (See Chart 3-5, p. 18.)

In (d) and (e): There is no difference in meaning between *After finishing* and *After having finished*.

(f)	Phrase:	Peter went to bed **after finishing** his homework.

The modifying adverbial phrase may follow the main clause, as in (f).

18-3 Expressing the Idea of "During the Same Time" in Modifying Adverbial Phrases

(a)	**While I was walking** down the street, *I* ran into an old friend.
(b)	**While walking** down the street, *I* ran into an old friend.
(c)	**Walking** down the street, *I* ran into an old friend.

Sometimes **while** is omitted, but the **-ing** phrase at the beginning of the sentence gives the same meaning (i.e., "during the same time").

Examples (a), (b), and (c) have the same meaning.

While George was resting on the beach, **he** fell asleep.
Resting on the beach, **George** fell asleep.

18-4 Expressing Cause and Effect in Modifying Adverbial Phrases

(a) *Because she needed* some money to buy a book, *Sue* cashed a check. (b) *Needing* some money to buy a book, *Sue* cashed a check. (c) *Because he lacked* the necessary qualifications, *he* was not considered for the job. (d) *Lacking* the necessary qualifications, *he* was not considered for the job.	Often an *-ing* phrase at the beginning of a sentence gives the meaning of "because." Examples (a) and (b) have the same meaning. *Because* is not included in a modifying phrase. It is omitted, but the resulting phrase expresses a cause-and-effect relationship, as in (b) and (d).
(e) *Having seen* that movie before, *I don't want* to go again. (f) *Having seen* that movie before, *I didn't want* to go again.	*Having* + *past participle* gives the meaning not only of "because" but also of "before."
(g) *Because she was unable* to afford a car, *she* bought a bicycle. (h) *Being unable* to afford a car, *she* bought a bicycle. (i) *Unable* to afford a car, *she* bought a bicycle.	A form of *be* in the adverb clause may be changed to *being*. The use of *being* makes the cause-and-effect relationship clear. Examples (g), (h), and (i) have the same meaning.

18-5 Using *Upon* + *-ing* in Modifying Adverbial Phrases

(a) *Upon reaching* the age of 21, I received my inheritance. (b) *When I reached* the age of 21, I received my inheritance.	Modifying adverbial phrases beginning with *upon* + *-ing* usually have the same meaning as adverb clauses introduced by *when*. Examples (a) and (b) have the same meaning.
(c) *On reaching* the age of 21, I received my inheritance.	*Upon* can be shortened to *on*. Examples (a), (b), and (c) all have the same meaning.

Chapter 19

Connectives That Express Cause and Effect, Contrast, and Condition

19-1 Using *Because Of* and *Due To*

(a) *Because* the weather was cold, we stayed home.	*Because* introduces an adverb clause; it is followed by a subject and a verb, as in (a).
(b) *Because of* the cold weather, we stayed home. (c) *Due to* the cold weather, we stayed home.	*Because of* and *due to* are phrasal prepositions; they are followed by a noun object, as in (b) and (c).
(d) *Due to the fact that* the weather was cold, we stayed home.	Sometimes (usually in more formal writing) *due to* is followed by a noun clause introduced by *the fact that*.
(e) We stayed home *because of the cold weather*. We stayed home *due to the cold weather*. We stayed home *due to the fact that the weather was cold*.	Like adverb clauses, these phrases can also follow the main clause, as in (e).

Because of the storm, we didn't go camping.

19-2 Cause and Effect: Using *Therefore, Consequently,* and *So*

(a) Al failed the test because he didn't study. (b) Al didn't study. ***Therefore,*** he failed the test. (c) Al didn't study. ***Consequently,*** he failed the test.	Examples (a), (b), and (c) have the same meaning. ***Therefore*** and ***consequently*** mean "as a result." In grammar, they are called *transitions* (or *conjunctive adverbs*). Transitions connect the ideas between two sentences. They are used most commonly in formal written English and rarely in spoken English.

(d) Al didn't study. ***Therefore,*** he failed the test.
(e) Al didn't study. He***, therefore,*** failed the test.
(f) Al didn't study. He failed the test***, therefore***.
 	
POSITIONS OF A TRANSITION:
transition + **S** + **V** (+ rest of sentence)
    S + ***transition*** + **V** (+ rest of sentence)
    S + **V** (+ rest of sentence) + ***transition***
	A transition occurs in the second of two related sentences.
	
	Notice the patterns and punctuation in the examples. A period (NOT a comma) is used at the end of the first sentence.* The transition has several positions in the second sentence. The transition is separated from the rest of the sentence by commas.

(g) Al didn't study***, so*** he failed the test.	In (g): ***So*** is used as a *conjunction* between two independent clauses. It has the same meaning as ***therefore***. ***So*** is common in both formal written and spoken English. A comma usually precedes ***so*** when it connects two sentences, as in (g).

*A semicolon is also possible in this situation. See the footnote to Chart 19-3.

The grocer needed to buy some stamps. ***Therefore,*** he left work for a few minutes to go to the post office.

19-3 Summary of Patterns and Punctuation

Adverb Clauses	(a) **Because** it was hot**,** we went swimming. (b) We went swimming **because** it was hot.	An *adverb clause* may precede or follow an independent clause. PUNCTUATION: A comma is used if the adverb clause comes first.
Prepositions	(c) **Because of** the hot weather**,** we went swimming. (d) We went swimming **because of** the hot weather.	A *preposition* is followed by a noun object, not by a subject and verb. PUNCTUATION: A comma is usually used if the prepositional phrase precedes the subject and verb of the independent clause.
Transitions	(e) It was hot. **Therefore,** we went swimming. (f) It was hot. We**, therefore,** went swimming. (g) It was hot. We went swimming**, therefore.**	A *transition* is used with the second sentence of a pair. It shows the relationship of the second idea to the first idea. A transition is movable within the second sentence. PUNCTUATION: A period is used between the two independent clauses.* A comma may NOT be used to separate the clauses. Commas are usually used to set the transition off from the rest of the sentence.
Conjunctions	(h) It was hot**, so** we went swimming.	A conjunction comes between two independent clauses. PUNCTUATION: Usually a comma is used immediately in front of a conjunction.

*A semicolon (;) may be used instead of a period between the two independent clauses.
    It was hot; therefore, we went swimming.
    It was hot; we, therefore, went swimming.
    It was hot; we went swimming, therefore.
In general, a semicolon can be used instead of a period between any two sentences that are closely related in meaning: *Peanuts are not nuts; they are beans.* Notice that a small letter, NOT a capital letter, immediately follows a semicolon.

19-4 Other Ways of Expressing Cause and Effect: *Such . . . That* and *So . . . That*

(a) Because the weather was nice, we went to the zoo. (b) It was *such nice weather that* we went to the zoo. (c) The weather was *so nice that* we went to the zoo.	Examples (a), (b), and (c) have the same meaning.
(d) It was *such good coffee that* I had another cup. (e) It was *such a foggy day that* we couldn't see the road.	*Such . . . that* encloses a modified noun: *such* + *adjective* + *noun* + *that*
(f) The coffee is *so hot that* I can't drink it. (g) I'm *so hungry that* I could eat a horse. (h) She speaks *so fast that* I can't understand her. (i) He walked *so quickly that* I couldn't keep up with him.	*So . . . that* encloses an adjective or adverb: *so* + $\left\{ \begin{array}{c} adjective \\ or \\ adverb \end{array} \right\}$ + *that*
(j) She made *so many mistakes that* she failed the exam. (k) He has *so few friends that* he is always lonely. (l) She has *so much money that* she can buy whatever she wants. (m) He had *so little trouble* with the test *that* he left twenty minutes early.	*So . . . that* is used with *many, few, much,* and *little.*
(n) It was *such a good book* (that) I couldn't put it down. (o) I was *so hungry* (that) I didn't wait for dinner to eat something.	Sometimes, primarily in speaking, *that* is omitted.

19-5 Expressing Purpose: Using *So That*

(a) I turned off the TV ***in order to*** enable my roommate to study in peace and quiet. (b) I turned off the TV ***so*** (***that***) my roommate could study in peace and quiet.	***In order to*** expresses *purpose*. (See Chart 15-1, p. 84.) In (a): I turned off the TV for a purpose. The purpose was to make it possible for my roommate to study in peace and quiet.

So That + *Can* or *Could*

(c) I'm going to cash a check ***so that I can*** buy my textbooks. (d) I cashed a check ***so that I could*** buy my textbooks.	***So that*** also expresses *purpose.** It expresses the same meaning as ***in order to***. The word "that" is often omitted, especially in speaking. ***So that*** is often used instead of ***in order to*** when the idea of ability is being expressed. ***Can*** is used in the adverb clause for a present/future meaning. In (c): ***so that I can buy*** = in order to be able to buy ***Could*** is used after ***so that*** in past sentences, as in (d).**

So That + *Will / Would* or **Simple Present**

(e) I'll take my umbrella ***so that I won't*** get wet. (f) Yesterday I took my umbrella ***so that I wouldn't*** get wet. (g) I'll take my umbrella ***so that I don't*** get wet.	In (e): ***so that I won't get wet*** = in order to make sure that I won't get wet ***Would*** is used in past sentences, as in (f). In (g): It is sometimes possible to use the simple present after ***so that*** in place of ***will***; the simple present expresses a future meaning.

*NOTE: *In order that* has the same meaning as *so that* but is less commonly used.
   Example: *I turned off the TV **in order that** my roommate could study in peace and quiet.*
  Both *so that* and *in order that* introduce adverb clauses. It is unusual but possible to put these adverb clauses at the beginning
  of a sentence: ***So that** my roommate could study in peace and quiet, I turned off the TV.*

Also possible but less common: the use of ***may* or ***might*** in place of ***can*** or ***could*** (e.g., *I cashed a check **so that I might** buy
   my textbooks.*).

He asked for help ***so that he could*** find a campsite.

19-6 Showing Contrast (Unexpected Result)

All of these sentences have the same meaning. The idea of cold weather is contrasted with the idea of going swimming. Usually if the weather is cold, one does not go swimming, so going swimming in cold weather is an "unexpected result." It is surprising that the speaker went swimming in cold weather.

Adverb Clauses	*even though* *although* *though*	(a) **Even though** it was cold, I went swimming. (b) **Although** it was cold, I went swimming. (c) **Though** it was cold, I went swimming.
Conjunctions	*but . . . anyway* *but . . . still* *yet . . . still*	(d) It was cold, **but** I went swimming **anyway**. (e) It was cold, **but** I **still** went swimming. (f) It was cold, **yet** I **still** went swimming.
Transitions	*nevertheless* *nonetheless* *however . . . still*	(g) It was cold. **Nevertheless**, I went swimming. (h) It was cold; **nonetheless**, I went swimming. (i) It was cold. **However**, I **still** went swimming.
Prepositions	*despite* *in spite of* *despite the fact that* *in spite of the fact that*	(j) I went swimming **despite** the cold weather. (k) I went swimming **in spite of** the cold weather. (l) I went swimming **despite the fact that** the weather was cold. (m) I went swimming **in spite of the fact that** the weather was cold.

19-7 Showing Direct Contrast

All of the sentences have the same meaning: "This" is the opposite of "that."

Adverb Clauses	*while*	(a) Mary is rich, **while** John is poor.* (b) John is poor, **while** Mary is rich.
Conjunctions	*but*	(c) Mary is rich, **but** John is poor. (d) John is poor, **but** Mary is rich.
Transitions	*however* *on the other hand*	(e) Mary is rich; **however**, John is poor. (f) John is poor; Mary is rich, **however**. (g) Mary is rich. John, **on the other hand**, is poor. (h) John is poor. Mary, **on the other hand**, is rich.

*Sometimes a comma precedes a *while*-clause that shows direct contrast. A comma helps clarify that *while* is being used to express contrast rather than time. The use of a comma in this instance is a stylistic choice by the writer.

19-8 Expressing Conditions: Using *Otherwise* and *Or (Else)*

Adverb Clauses	(a) *If* I don't eat breakfast, I get hungry. (b) You'll be late *if* you don't hurry. (c) You'll get wet *unless* you take your umbrella.	*If* and *unless* state conditions that produce certain results. (See Charts 17-6 and 17-10, pp. 93 and 94.)
Transitions	(d) I always eat breakfast. *Otherwise,* I get hungry during class. (e) You'd better hurry. *Otherwise,* you'll be late. (f) Take your umbrella. *Otherwise,* you'll get wet.	*Otherwise* expresses the idea "if the opposite is true, then there will be a certain result." In (d): *otherwise = if I don't eat breakfast*
Conjunctions	(g) I always eat breakfast, *or (else)* I get hungry during class. (h) You'd better hurry, *or (else)* you'll be late. (i) Take your umbrella, *or (else)* you'll get wet.	*Or else* and *otherwise* have the same meaning.

19-9 Summary of Connectives: Cause and Effect, Contrast, and Condition

	Adverb Clause Words		Transitions	Conjunctions	Prepositions
Cause and Effect	because since now that	so (that)	therefore consequently	so	because of due to
Contrast	even though although though	while	however nevertheless nonetheless on the other hand	but (. . . anyway) yet (. . . still)	despite in spite of
Condition	if unless only if even if whether or not	in case	otherwise	or (else)	

Chapter 20
Conditional Sentences and Wishes

20-1 Overview of Basic Verb Forms Used in Conditional Sentences

Situation	*If*-clause	Result clause	Examples
True in the Present/Future	simple present	*will* + *simple form*	If I *have* enough time, I *watch* TV every evening. If I *have* enough time, I *will watch* TV later on tonight.
Untrue in the Present/Future	simple past	*would* + *simple form*	If I *had* enough time, I *would watch* TV now or later on.
Untrue in the Past	past perfect	*would have* + *past participle*	If I *had had* enough time, I *would have watched* TV yesterday.

20-2 True in the Present or Future

(a) If I *don't eat* breakfast, I always *get* hungry during class.

(b) Water *freezes* OR *will freeze* if the temperature *reaches* 32°F/0°C.

(c) If I *don't eat* breakfast tomorrow morning, I *will get* hungry during class.

(d) If it *rains*, we *should stay* home.
If it *rains*, I *might decide* to stay home.
If it *rains*, we *can't go*.
If it *rains*, we *'re going to stay* home.

(e) If anyone *calls*, please *take* a message.

In conditional sentences that express true, factual ideas in the present/future, the *simple present* (not the simple future) is used in the *if*-clause.

The result clause has various possible verb forms. A result clause verb can be:

- the *simple present,* to express a habitual activity or situation, as in (a).
- either the *simple present* or the *simple future,* to express an established, predictable fact or general truth, as in (b).
- the *simple future,* to express a particular activity or situation in the future, as in (c).
- *modals* and *phrasal modals* such as ***should, might, can, be going to,*** as in (d).*
- an *imperative* verb, as in (e).

(f) If anyone *should* call, please take a message.

Sometimes ***should*** is used in an *if*-clause. It indicates a little more uncertainty than the use of the simple present, but basically the meaning of examples (e) and (f) is the same.

*See Chart 9-1, p. 42, for a list of modals and phrasal modals.

20-3 Untrue (Contrary to Fact) in the Present or Future

(a) If I *taught* this class, I *wouldn't give* tests.	In (a): In truth, I don't teach this class.
(b) If he *were* here right now, he *would help* us.	In (b): In truth, he is not here right now.
(c) If I *were* you, I *would accept* their invitation.	In (c): In truth, I am not you.
	NOTE: *Were* is used for both singular and plural subjects. *Was* (with *I, he, she, it*) is sometimes used in informal speech: *If I was you, I'd accept their invitation.*
COMPARE: (d) If I had enough money, I *would* buy a car. (e) If I had enough money, I *could* buy a car.	In (d): The speaker wants a car but doesn't have enough money. *Would* expresses desired or predictable results. In (e): The speaker is expressing one possible result. *could* = *would be able to; could* expresses possible options.

20-4 Untrue (Contrary to Fact) in the Past

(a) If you *had told* me about the problem, I *would have helped* you.	In (a): In truth, you did not tell me about it.
(b) If they *had studied*, they *would have passed* the exam.	In (b): In truth, they did not study. Therefore, they failed the exam.
(c) If I *hadn't slipped* on the stairs, I *wouldn't have broken* my arm.	In (c): In truth, I slipped on the stairs. I broke my arm. NOTE: The auxiliary verbs are often reduced in speech. "If you'd told me, I would've helped you (OR *I-duv* helped you)."*
COMPARE: (d) If I had had enough money, I *would* have bought a car. (e) If I had had enough money, I *could* have bought a car.	In (d): *would* expresses a desired or predictable result. In (e): *could* expresses a possible option. *could have bought* = *would have been able to buy*

*In casual, informal speech, some native speakers sometimes use **would have** in an *if*-clause: *If you **would've told** me about the problem, I would've helped you.* This verb form usage is generally considered to be grammatically incorrect in standard English, but it occurs fairly commonly.

If Elena **had heard** the phone ring,
she **would have answered** it.

20-5 Using Progressive Verb Forms in Conditional Sentences

Notice the use of progressive verb forms in these examples. Even in conditional sentences, progressive verb forms are used in progressive situations. (See Chart 1-2, p. 2, for a discussion of progressive verbs.)

(a)	True:	It *is raining* right now, so I *will not go* for a walk.
(b)	Conditional:	If it *were not raining* right now, I *would go* for a walk.

(c)	True:	It *was raining* yesterday afternoon, so I *did not go* for a walk.
(d)	Conditional:	If it *had not been raining,* I *would have gone* for a walk.

20-6 Using "Mixed Time" in Conditional Sentences

Frequently the time in the *if*-clause and the time in the result clause are different: one clause may be in the present and the other in the past. Notice that past and present times are mixed in these sentences.

(a)	True:	I *did not eat* breakfast several hours ago, so I *am* hungry now.
(b)	Conditional:	If I *had eaten* breakfast several hours ago, I *would not be* hungry now.
		(past) (present)

(c)	True:	He *is not* a good student. He *did not study* for the test yesterday.
(d)	Conditional:	If he *were* a good student, he *would have studied* for the test yesterday.
		(present) (past)

20-7 Omitting *If*

(a) *Were I* you, I wouldn't do that.	With *were, had* (past perfect), and *should*, sometimes *if* is omitted and the subject and verb are inverted.
(b) *Had I known,* I would have told you.	In (a): *Were I you* = if I were you
(c) *Should anyone call,* please take a message.	In (b): *Had I known* = if I had known
	In (c): *Should anyone call* = if anyone should call

20-8 Implied Conditions

(a) I *would have gone* with you, *but I had to study.* (b) I never *would have succeeded* without your help.	Often the *if*-clause is implied, not stated. Conditional verbs are still used in the result clause. In (a): the implied condition = *if I hadn't had to study* In (b): the implied condition = *if you hadn't helped me*
(c) She ran; *otherwise, she would have missed* her bus.	Conditional verbs are frequently used following **otherwise**. In (c), the implied *if*-clause = *if she had not run*

20-9 Verb Forms Following *Wish*

Wish is used when the speaker wants reality to be different, to be exactly the opposite.

	"True" Statement	Verb Form Following *Wish*	
A Wish about the Future	(a) She *will not tell* me. (b) He *isn't going to be* here. (c) She *can't come* tomorrow.	I *wish* (that) she *would tell* me. I *wish* he *were going to be* here. I *wish* she *could come* tomorrow.	**Wish** is followed by a noun clause. (See Chart 12-5, p. 65.) Past verb forms, similar to those in conditional sentences, are used in the noun clause.
A Wish about the Present	(d) I *don't know* French. (e) It *is raining* right now. (f) I *can't speak* Japanese.	I *wish* I *knew* French. I *wish* it *weren't raining* right now. I *wish* I *could speak* Japanese.	For example, in (a): **would**, the past form of **will**, is used to make a wish about the future. In (d): the simple past (**knew**) is used to make a wish about the present.
A Wish about the Past	(g) John *didn't come*. (h) Mary *couldn't come*.	I *wish* John *had come*.* I *wish* Mary *could have come*.	In (g): the past perfect (**had come**) is used to make a wish about the past.

*Sometimes in very informal speaking: *I wish John **would have** come.*

20-10 Using *Would* to Make Wishes about the Future

(a) It is raining. I *wish* it *would stop*. (*I want it to stop raining.*) (b) I'm expecting a call. I *wish* the phone *would ring*. (*I want the phone to ring.*)	**Would** is usually used to indicate that the speaker wants something to happen or someone other than the speaker to do something in the future. The wish may or may not come true (be realized).
(c) It's going to be a good party. I *wish* you *would come*. (d) We're going to be late. I *wish* you *would hurry*.	In (c) and (d): **I wish you would** . . . is often used to make a request.

Appendix
Supplementary Grammar Charts

UNIT A: Basic Grammar Terminology

A-1 Subjects, Verbs, and Objects

(a) <u>Birds</u> <u>fly</u>.
   (noun) (verb)
   S   **V**
	Almost all English sentences contain a subject (**S**) and a verb (**V**). The verb may or may not be followed by an object (**O**).

(b) The <u>baby</u> <u>cried</u>.
     (noun) (verb)
      S   **V**
	VERBS: Verbs that are not followed by an object, as in (a) and (b), are called "intransitive verbs."
	Common intransitive verbs: *agree, arrive, come, cry, exist, go, happen, live, occur, rain, rise, sleep, stay, walk.*

(c) The <u>student</u> <u>needs</u> a <u>pen</u>.
     (noun)   (verb) (noun)
      S   **V**   **O**
	Verbs that are followed by an object, as in (c) and (d), are called "transitive verbs."
	Common transitive verbs: *build, cut, find, like, make, need, send, use, want.*

(d) My <u>friend</u> <u>enjoyed</u> the <u>party</u>.
     (noun)   (verb)   (noun)
      S   **V**   **O**
	Some verbs can be either intransitive or transitive.
	  Intransitive: *A student studies.*
	  Transitive: *A student studies books.*

	SUBJECTS AND OBJECTS: The subjects and objects of verbs are nouns (or pronouns). Examples of nouns: *person, place, thing, John, Asia, pen, information, appearance, amusement.*

A-2 Adjectives

(a) Ann is an ***intelligent*** *student*.
          (adjective) (noun)
(b) The ***hungry*** *child* ate fruit.
    (adjective) (noun)
	Adjectives describe nouns. In grammar, we say that adjectives modify nouns. The word *modify* means "change a little." Adjectives give a little different meaning to a noun: *intelligent student, lazy student, good student.*
	Examples of adjectives: *young, old, rich, beautiful, brown, French, modern.*

(c) I saw some ***beautiful*** *pictures*. *INCORRECT:* beautiful~~s~~ pictures	An adjective is neither singular nor plural. A final **-s** is never added to an adjective.

A-3 Adverbs

(a) He walks *quickly*.
    (adverb)
 	
(b) She opened the door *quietly*.
    (adverb)
	Adverbs modify verbs. Often they answer the question "How?"
	
	In (a): *How does he walk?* Answer: *Quickly.*
	
	Adverbs are often formed by adding **-ly** to an adjective.
	    Adjective: *quick*
	    Adverb: *quickly*

(c) I am *extremely happy*. (adverb) (adjective)	Adverbs are also used to modify adjectives, i.e., to give information about adjectives, as in (c).
(d) Ann will come *tomorrow*. (adverb)	Adverbs are also used to express time or frequency. Examples: *tomorrow, today, yesterday, soon, never, usually, always, yet.*
MIDSENTENCE ADVERBS: (e) Ann *always comes* on time. (f) Ann *is always* on time. (g) Ann *has always come* on time. (h) *Does she always come* on time?	Some adverbs may occur in the middle of a sentence. Midsentence adverbs have usual positions; they • come in front of simple present and simple past verbs (except **be**), as in (e); • follow **be** (simple present and simple past), as in (f); • come between a helping verb and a main verb, as in (g). In a question, a midsentence adverb comes directly after the subject, as in (h).

Common midsentence adverbs

ever always	usually often frequently	generally sometimes occasionally	seldom rarely hardly ever	never not ever	already finally just probably

A-4 Prepositions and Prepositional Phrases

Common prepositions

about	at	beyond	into	since	up
above	before	by	like	through	upon
across	behind	despite	near	throughout	with
after	below	down	of	till	within
against	beneath	during	off	to	without
along	beside	for	on	toward(s)	
among	besides	from	out	under	
around	between	in	over	until	

S   **V**   **PREP** **O of PREP**
(a) The ⌐student⌐ ⌐studies⌐ ⌐in⌐ the ⌐library.⌐
                             (noun)
 	
     S   **V**   **O** **PREP**   **O of PREP**
(b) ⌐We⌐ ⌐enjoyed⌐ the ⌐party⌐ ⌐at⌐ your ⌐house.⌐
                               (noun)
	An important element of English sentences is the prepositional phrase. It consists of a preposition (**PREP**) and its object (**o**). The object of a preposition is a noun or pronoun.
	
	In (a): *in the library* is a prepositional phrase.

(c) We went *to the zoo* *in the afternoon*. (Place) (Time) (d) *In the afternoon,* we went to the zoo.	In (c): In most English sentences, "place" comes before "time." In (d): Sometimes a prepositional phrase comes at the beginning of a sentence.

A-5 The Verb *Be*

(a) John **is** *a student*. 　　　(be)　(noun) (b) John **is** *intelligent*. 　　　(be)　(adjective) (c) John **was** *at the library*. 　　　(be)　(prep. phrase)	A sentence with **be** as the main verb has three basic patterns: 　In (a): **be** + *a noun* 　In (b): **be** + *an adjective* 　In (c): **be** + *a prepositional phrase*
(d) Mary **is** *writing* a letter. (e) They **were** *listening* to some music. (f) That letter **was** *written* by Alice.	**Be** is also used as an auxiliary verb in progressive verb tenses and in the passive. 　In (d): **is** = *auxiliary*; **writing** = *main verb*

Tense Forms of *Be*

	SIMPLE PRESENT	SIMPLE PAST	PRESENT PERFECT
Singular	*I am* *you are* *he, she, it is*	*I was* *you were* *he, she, it was*	*I have been* *you have been* *he, she, it has been*
Plural	*we, you, they are*	*we, you, they were*	*we, you, they have been*

A-6 Linking Verbs

(a) The soup　**smells**　**good**. 　　　(linking verb) (adjective) (b) This food **tastes delicious**. (c) The children **feel happy**. (d) The weather **became cold**.	Other verbs like **be** that may be followed immediately by an adjective are called "linking verbs." An adjective following a linking verb describes the subject of a sentence.* Common verbs that may be followed by an adjective: 　• *feel, look, smell, sound, taste* 　• *appear, seem* 　• *become* (and *get, turn, grow* when they mean "become")

*COMPARE:
　(1) *The man looks angry.* → An adjective (**angry**) follows **look**. The adjective describes the subject (**the man**). **Look** has the meaning of "appear."
　(2) *The man looked at me angrily.* → An adverb (**angrily**) follows **look at**. The adverb describes the action of the verb. **Look at** has the meaning of "regard, watch."

Ann *is* **at the laudromat**.
She **looks** very **busy**.

UNIT B: Questions

B-1 Forms of Yes/No and Information Questions

A yes/no question = a question that may be answered by *yes* or *no*	A: Does he live in Chicago? B: Yes, he does. OR No, he doesn't.

An information question = a question that asks for information by using a question word	A: Where does he live? B: In Chicago.

Question word order = (*Question word*) + *helping verb* + *subject* + *main verb*

Notice that the same subject-verb order is used in both yes/no and information questions.

(Question Word)	Helping Verb	Subject	Main Verb	(Rest of Sentence)	
(a) (b) Where	Does does	she she	live live?	there?	If the verb is in the simple present, use **does** (with *he, she, it*) or **do** (with *I, you, we, they*) in the question. If the verb is simple past, use **did**. Notice: The main verb in the question is in its simple form; there is no final *-s* or *-ed*.
(c) (d) Where	Do do	they they	live live?	there?	
(e) (f) Where	Did did	he he	live live?	there?	
(g) (h) Where	Is is	he he	living living?	there?	If the verb has an auxiliary (a helping verb), the same auxiliary is used in the question. There is no change in the form of the main verb. If the verb has more than one auxiliary, only the first auxiliary precedes the subject, as in (m) and (n).
(i) (j) Where	Have have	they they	lived lived?	there?	
(k) (l) Where	Can can	Mary Mary	live live?	there?	
(m) (n) Where	Will will	he he	be living be living?	there?	
(o) Who (p) Who	Ø can	Ø Ø	lives come?	there?	If the question word is the subject, usual question-word order is not used; **does, do,** and **did** are not used. The verb is in the same form in a question as it is in a statement. Statement: *Tom came.* Question: *Who came?*
(q) (r) Where	Are are	they they?	Ø Ø	there?	Main verb **be** in the simple present (*am, is, are*) and simple past (*was, were*) precedes the subject. It has the same position as a helping verb.
(s) (t) Where	Was was	Jim Jim?	Ø Ø	there?	

B-2 Question Words

	Question	Answer	
When	(a) **When** did they arrive? **When** will you come?	Yesterday. Next Monday.	**When** is used to ask questions about *time*.
Where	(b) **Where** is she? **Where** can I find a pen?	At home. In that drawer.	**Where** is used to ask questions about *place*.
Why	(c) **Why** did he leave early? **Why** aren't you coming with us?	Because he's ill. I'm tired.	**Why** is used to ask questions about *reason*.
How	(d) **How** did you come to school? **How** does he drive?	By bus. Carefully.	**How** generally asks about *manner*.
	(e) **How much** money does it cost? **How many** people came?	Ten dollars. Fifteen.	**How** is used with **much** and **many**.
	(f) **How old** are you? **How cold** is it? **How soon** can you get here? **How fast** were you driving?	Twelve. Ten below zero. In ten minutes. 50 miles an hour.	**How** is also used with adjectives and adverbs.
	(g) **How long** has he been here? **How often** do you write home? **How far** is it to Miami from here?	Two years. Every week. 500 miles.	**How long** asks about *length of time*. **How often** asks about *frequency*. **How far** asks about *distance*.
Who	(h) **Who** can answer that question? **Who** came to visit you?	I can. Jane and Eric.	**Who** is used as the subject of a question. It refers to people.
	(i) **Who** is coming to dinner tonight? **Who** wants to come with me?	Ann, Bob, and Al. We do.	**Who** is usually followed by a singular verb even if the speaker is asking about more than one person.
Whom	(j) **Who(m)** did you see? **Who(m)** are you visiting?	I saw George. My relatives.	**Whom** is used as the object of a verb or preposition. In everyday spoken English, **whom** is rarely used; **who** is used instead. **Whom** is used only in formal questions.
	(k) **Who(m)** should I talk *to*? *To* **whom** should I talk? (formal)	The secretary.	NOTE: **Whom**, not **who**, is used if preceded by a preposition.
Whose	(l) **Whose** book did you borrow? **Whose** key is this? (**Whose** is this?)	David's. It's mine.	**Whose** asks questions about *possession*.

	Question	**Answer**	
What	(m) *What* made you angry? *What* went wrong?	His rudeness. Everything.	***What*** is used as the subject of a question. It refers to things.
	(n) *What* do you need? *What* did Alice buy?	I need a pencil. A book.	***What*** is also used as an object.
	(o) *What* did he talk *about*? *About* **what** did he talk? (formal)	His vacation.	
	(p) *What kind of* soup is that? *What kind of* shoes did he buy?	It's bean soup. Sandals.	***What kind of*** asks about the particular variety or type of something.
	(q) *What did* you *do* last night? *What is* Mary *doing*?	I studied. Reading a book.	***What*** + *a form of* ***do*** is used to ask questions about activities.
	(r) *What countries* did you visit? *What time* did she come? *What color* is his hair?	Italy and Spain. Seven o'clock. Dark brown.	***What*** may accompany a noun.
	(s) *What is* Ed *like*?	He's kind and friendly.	***What*** + ***be like*** asks for a general description of qualities.
	(t) *What is* the weather *like*?	Hot and humid.	
	(u) *What does* Ed *look like*?	He's tall and has dark hair.	***What*** + ***look like*** asks for a physical description.
	(v) *What does* her house *look like*?	It's a two-story,* red brick house.	
Which	(w) I have two pens. *Which pen* do you want? *Which one* do you want? *Which do* you want?	The blue one.	***Which*** is used instead of ***what*** when a question concerns choosing from a definite, known quantity or group.
	(x) *Which book* should I buy?	That one.	
	(y) *Which countries* did he visit? *What countries* did he visit?	Peru and Chile.	In some cases, there is little difference in meaning between ***which*** and ***what*** when they accompany a noun, as in (y) and (z).
	(z) *Which class* are you in? *What class* are you in?	This class.	

*American English: *a two-**story** house.*
British English: *a two-**storey** house.*

B-3 Shortened Yes/No Questions

(a) *Going to bed now?* = *Are you going to bed now?* (b) *Finish your work?* = *Did you finish your work?* (c) *Want to go to the movie with us?* = *Do you want to go to the movie with us?*	Sometimes in spoken English, the auxiliary and the subject *you* are dropped from a yes/no question, as in (a), (b), and (c).

B-4 Negative Questions

(a) *Doesn't she live* in the dormitory? (b) *Does she not live* in the dormitory? (very formal)	In a yes/no question in which the verb is negative, usually a contraction (e.g., *does* + *not* = *doesn't*) is used, as in (a). Example (b) is very formal and is usually not used in everyday speech. Negative questions are used to indicate the speaker's idea (i.e., what she/he believes is or is not true) or attitude (e.g., surprise, shock, annoyance, anger).
(c) Bob returns to his dorm room after his nine o'clock class. Matt, his roommate, is there. Bob is surprised. Bob says, "*What are you doing here? Aren't you supposed to be in class now?*"	In (c): Bob believes that Matt is supposed to be in class now. *Expected answer:* **Yes**.
(d) Alice and Mary are at home. Mary is about to leave on a trip, and Alice is going to take her to the airport. Alice says, "*It's already two o'clock. We'd better leave for the airport. Doesn't your plane leave at three?*"	In (d): Alice believes that Mary's plane leaves at three. She is asking the negative question to make sure that her information is correct. *Expected answer:* **Yes**.
(e) The teacher is talking to Jim about a test he failed. The teacher is surprised that Jim failed the test because he usually does very well. The teacher says: "*What happened? Didn't you study?*"	In (e): The teacher believes that Jim did not study. *Expected answer:* **No**.
(f) Barb and Ron are riding in a car. Ron is driving. He comes to a corner where there is a stop sign, but he does not stop the car. Barb is shocked. Barb says, "*What's the matter with you? Didn't you see that stop sign?*"	In (f): Barb believes that Ron did not see the stop sign. *Expected answer:* **No**.

B-5 Tag Questions

(a) Jack *can* come, *can't* he? (b) Fred *can't* come, *can* he?	A tag question is a question added at the end of a sentence. Speakers use tag questions mainly to make sure their information is correct or to seek agreement.*

AFFIRMATIVE SENTENCE + NEGATIVE TAG → AFFIRMATIVE ANSWER EXPECTED

Mary *is* here,	*isn't* she?	Yes, she is.
You *like* tea,	*don't* you?	Yes, I do.
They *have left*,	*haven't* they?	Yes, they have.

NEGATIVE SENTENCE + AFFIRMATIVE TAG → NEGATIVE ANSWER EXPECTED

Mary *isn't* here,	*is* she?	No, she isn't.
You *don't like* tea,	*do* you?	No, I don't.
They *haven't left,*	*have* they?	No, they haven't.

(c) *This/That* is your book, isn't *it*? *These/Those* are yours, aren't *they*?	The tag pronoun for ***this/that*** = ***it***. The tag pronoun for ***these/those*** = ***they***.
(d) *There is* a meeting tonight, *isn't there*?	In sentences with ***there + be***, ***there*** is used in the tag.
(e) *Everything* is okay, isn't *it*? (f) *Everyone* took the test, didn't *they*?	Personal pronouns are used to refer to indefinite pronouns. ***They*** is usually used in a tag to refer to ***everyone***, ***everybody***, ***someone***, ***somebody***, ***no one***, ***nobody***.
(g) *Nothing is* wrong, *is* it? (h) *Nobody called* on the phone, *did* they? (i) You*'ve never been* there, *have* you?	Sentences with negative words take affirmative tags.
(j) *I am* supposed to be here, *am I not*? (k) *I am* supposed to be here, *aren't I*?	In (j): ***am I not?*** is formal English. In (k): ***aren't I?*** is common in spoken English.

*A tag question may be spoken:
  (1) with a rising intonation if the speaker is truly seeking to ascertain that his/her information, idea, belief is correct (e.g., *Ann lives in an apartment, doesn't she?*); OR
  (2) with a falling intonation if the speaker is expressing an idea with which she/he is almost certain the listener will agree (e.g., *It's a nice day today, isn't it?*).

Jim ***could*** use some help, ***couldn't*** he?

UNIT C: Contractions

C Contractions

IN SPEAKING: In everyday spoken English, certain forms of **be** and auxiliary verbs are usually contracted with pronouns, nouns, and question words.

IN WRITING: (1) In written English, contractions with pronouns are common in informal writing, but they're not generally acceptable in formal writing.

(2) Contractions with nouns and question words are, for the most part, rarely used in writing. A few of these contractions may be found in quoted dialogue in stories or in very informal writing, such as a chatty letter to a good friend, but most of them are rarely if ever written.

In the following, quotation marks indicate that the contraction is frequently spoken but rarely, if ever, written.

	With Pronouns	**With Nouns**	**With Question Words**
am	*I'm* reading a book.	Ø	*"What'm"* I supposed to do?
is	*She's* studying. *It's* going to rain.	My *"book's"* on the table. *Mary's* at home.	*Where's* Sally? *Who's* that man?
are	*You're* working hard. *They're* waiting for us.	My *"books're"* on the table. The *"teachers're"* at a meeting.	*"What're"* you doing? *"Where're"* they going?
has	*She's* been here for a year. *It's* been cold lately.	My *"book's"* been stolen! *Sally's* never met him.	*Where's* Sally been living? *What's* been going on?
have	*I've* finished my work. *They've* never met you.	The *"books've"* been sold. The *"students've"* finished the test.	*"Where've"* they been? *"How've"* you been?
had	*He'd* been waiting for us. *We'd* forgotten about it.	The *"books'd"* been sold. *"Mary'd"* never met him before.	*"Where'd"* you been before that? *"Who'd"* been there before you?
did	Ø	Ø	*"What'd"* you do last night? *"How'd"* you do on the test?
will	*I'll* come later. *She'll* help us.	The *"weather'll"* be nice tomorrow. *"John'll"* be coming soon.	*"Who'll"* be at the meeting? *"Where'll"* you be at ten?
would	*He'd* like to go there. *They'd* come if they could.	My *"friends'd"* come if they could. *"Mary'd"* like to go there too.	*"Where'd"* you like to go?

UNIT D: Negatives

D-1 Using *Not* and Other Negative Words

(a) AFFIRMATIVE: The earth is round. (b) NEGATIVE: The earth is *not* flat.	*Not* expresses a *negative* idea.

AUX + *NOT* + MAIN VERB
 (c) I *will*   *not*   *go*   there.
      I *have* *not* *gone*   there.
      I *am*   *not* *going*   there.
      I *was*   *not*   there.
      I *do*   *not* *go*   there.
   He *does* *not* *go*   there.
      I *did*   *not* *go*   there.
	Not immediately follows an auxiliary verb or *be*.
	
	 NOTE: If there is more than one auxiliary, *not* comes immediately after the first auxiliary: *I **will not be** going there.*
	
	 Do or ***does*** is used with *not* to make a simple present verb (except *be*) negative.
	
	 Did is used with *not* to make a simple past verb (except *be*) negative.

Contractions of auxiliary verbs with *not*

are not = aren't* cannot = can't could not = couldn't did not = didn't does not = doesn't do not = don't	has not = hasn't have not = haven't had not = hadn't is not = isn't must not = mustn't should not = shouldn't	was not = wasn't were not = weren't will not = won't would not = wouldn't

(d) I almost *never* go there.
      I have *hardly ever* gone there.
	In addition to *not*, the following are negative adverbs:
	     never, rarely, seldom
	     hardly (ever), scarcely (ever), barely (ever)

(e) There's *no* chalk in the drawer.	*No* also expresses a negative idea.

COMPARE: *NOT* VS. *NO* (f) I *do not have* any money. (g) I have *no money*.	*Not* is used to make a verb negative, as in (f). *No* is used as an adjective in front of a noun (e.g., *money*), as in (g). NOTE: Examples (f) and (g) have the same meaning.

*Sometimes in spoken English you will hear "ain't." It means "am not," "isn't," or "aren't." *Ain't* is not considered proper English, but many people use *ain't* regularly, and it is also frequently used for humor.

D-2 Avoiding Double Negatives

(a) INCORRECT: I ~~don't~~ have ~~no~~ money.	Sentence (a) is an example of a "double negative," i.e., a confusing and grammatically incorrect sentence that contains two negatives in the same clause. One clause should contain only one negative.*
(b) CORRECT: I *don't* have *any money*. CORRECT: I have *no money*.	

*Negatives in two different clauses in the same sentence cause no problems; for example:
   *A person who **doesn't** have love **can't** be truly happy.*
   *I **don't** know why he **isn't** here.*

D-3 Beginning a Sentence with a Negative Word

(a) *Never will I do* that again! (b) *Rarely have I eaten* better food. (c) *Hardly ever does he come* to class on time.	When a negative word begins a sentence, the subject and verb are inverted (i.e., question word order is used).*

*Beginning a sentence with a negative word is relatively uncommon in everyday usage; it is used when the speaker/writer wishes to emphasize the negative element of the sentence and be expressive.

UNIT E: Preposition Combinations

E Preposition Combinations with Adjectives and Verbs

A
be absent from
be accused of
be accustomed to
be acquainted with
be addicted to
be afraid of
   agree with
be angry at, with
be annoyed with, by
   apologize for
   apply to, for
   approve of
   argue with, about
   arrive in, at
be associated with
be aware of

B
   believe in
   blame for
be blessed with
be bored with, by

C
be capable of
   care about, for
be cluttered with
be committed to
   compare to, with
   complain about, of
be composed of
be concerned about
be connected to
   consist of
be content with
   contribute to
be convinced of
be coordinated with
   count (up)on
be covered with
be crowded with

D
   decide (up)on
be dedicated to
   depend (up)on
be devoted to
be disappointed in, with
be discriminated against
   distinguish from
be divorced from
be done with

   dream of, about
be dressed in

E
be engaged in, to
be envious of
be equipped with
   escape from
   excel in, at
be excited about
   excuse for
be exhausted from
be exposed to

F
be faithful to
be familiar with
   feel like
   fight for
be filled with
be finished with
be fond of
   forget about
   forgive for
be friendly to, with
be frightened of, by
be furnished with

G
be gone from
be grateful to, for
be guilty of

H
   hide from
   hope for

I
be innocent of
   insist (up)on
be interested in
   introduce to
be involved in

J
be jealous of

K
   keep from
be known for

L
be limited to
be located in
   look forward to

M
be made of, from
be married to

O
   object to
be opposed to

P
   participate in
be patient with
be pleased with
be polite to
   pray for
be prepared for
   prevent from
   prohibit from
be protected from
be proud of
   provide with

Q
be qualified for

R
   recover from
be related to
be relevant to
   rely (up)on
be remembered for
   rescue from
   respond to
be responsible for

S
be satisfied with
be scared of, by
   stare at
   stop from
   subscribe to
   substitute for
   succeed in

T
   take advantage of
   take care of
   talk about, of
be terrified of, by
   thank for
   think about, of
be tired of, from

U
be upset with
be used to

V
   vote for

W
be worried about

UNIT F: The Subjunctive in Noun Clauses

F Using the Subjunctive in Noun Clauses

(a) The teacher *demands* that we *be* on time.	A subjunctive verb uses the simple form of a verb. It does not have present, past, or future forms; it is neither singular nor plural.
(b) I *insisted* that he *pay* me the money.	
(c) I *recommended* that she *not go* to the concert.	Sentences with subjunctive verbs generally *stress importance or urgency.* A subjunctive verb is used in *that*-clauses that follow the verbs and expressions listed below.
(d) *It is important* that they *be told* the truth.	In (a): *be* is a subjunctive verb; its subject is *we*.
	In (b): *pay* (not *pays*, not *paid*) is a subjunctive verb; it is in its simple form, even though its subject (*he*) is singular.
	Negative: *not* + *simple form,* as in (c).
	Passive: *simple form of **be*** + *past participle,* as in (d).
(e) I *suggested* that she *see* a doctor.	***Should*** is also possible after ***suggest*** and ***recommend.*** *
(f) I *suggested* that she *should see* a doctor.	

Common verbs and expressions followed by the subjunctive in a noun clause

advise (that)	propose (that)	it is critical (that)	it is important (that)
ask (that)	recommend (that)	it is essential (that)	it is necessary (that)
demand (that)	request (that)	it is imperative (that)	it is vital (that)
insist (that)	suggest (that)		

*The subjunctive is more common in American English than British English. In British English, ***should*** + *simple form* is more usual than the subjunctive: *The teacher **insists** that we **should be** on time.*

UNIT G: Troublesome Verbs

G Raise / Rise, Set / Sit, Lay / Lie

Transitive	Intransitive	
(a) *raise, raised, raised* Tom *raised* his hand.	(b) *rise, rose, risen* The sun *rises* in the east.	***Raise, set,*** and ***lay*** are *transitive* verbs; they are followed by an object. ***Rise, sit,*** and ***lie*** are *intransitive;* they are NOT followed by an object.*
(c) *set, set, set* I *will set* the book on the desk.	(d) *sit, sat, sat* I *sit* in the front row.	In (a): ***raised*** is followed by the object ***hand***. In (b): ***rises*** is not followed by an object.

(e) *lay, laid, laid*
I *am laying* the book on the desk.
	(f) *lie,** lay, lain*
	He *is lying* on his bed.
		NOTE: ***Lay*** and ***lie*** are troublesome for native speakers too and are frequently misused.
		    lay = put
		    lie = recline

*See Appendix Chart A-1 for information about transitive and intransitive verbs.

Lie is a regular verb (*lie, lied*) when it means "not tell the truth": *He **lied to me about his age.*

Index

Able to, 55, 57 *(Look on pages 55 and 57.)*	The numbers following the words listed in the index refer to page numbers in the text.
Continuous tenses, 2*fn.* *(Look at the footnote on page 2.)*	The letters *fn.* mean "footnote." Footnotes are at the bottom of a chart.

NOTES

NOTES

NOTES

NOTES

NOTES

NOTES